CONVERGENCE IN EVOLUTION • ARTHUR WILLE

Publisher's Note

The book descriptions we ask booksellers to display prominently warn that this is an historic book with numerous typos or missing text; it is not indexed or illustrated.

The book was created using optical character recognition software. The software is 99 percent accurate if the book is in good condition. However, we do understand that even one percent can be an annoying number of typos! And sometimes all or part of a page may be missing from the book. Or the paper may be so discolored from age that it is difficult to read. We apologize and gratefully acknowledge Google's assistance.

After we re-typeset and design a book, the page numbers change so the old index and table of contents no longer work. Therefore, we usually remove them.

Our books sell so few copies that you would have to pay hundreds of dollars to cover the cost of proof reading and fixing the typos, missing text and index. Therefore, whenever possible, we let our customers download a free copy of the original typo-free scanned book. Simply enter the barcode number from the back cover of the paperback in the Free Book form at www.general-books. net. You may also qualify for a free trial membership in our book club to download up to four books for free. Simply enter the barcode number from the back cover onto the membership form on the same page. The book club entitles you to select from more than a million books at no additional charge. Simply enter the title or subject onto the search form to find the books.

If you have any questions, could you please be so kind as to consult our Frequently Asked Questions page at www. general-books.net/faqs.cfm? You are also welcome to contact us there.

General Books LLC™, Memphis, USA, 2012. ISBN: 9780217823128.

❧ ❧ ❧ ❧ ❧ ❧ ❧ ❧

CONVERGENCE IN EVOLUTION CHAPTER I THE ART OF MORPHOLOGY, BEING A DISCOURSE UPON ORGANIC FORM

Morphology, in the modern sense, usually conveys a genetic meaning, implying morphogeny or the origin of forms. Its purpose is to follow the clue of affinity which connects related but divergent classes of animals and systems of organs, and to recognise primary forms when disguised beneath secondary facies. It is the handmaiden of comparative anatomy which is a much older discipline, the offspring of human anatomy and physiology, born in the schools of Vesalius, Fabricius ab Aquapedente, William Harvey and Malpighi. Morphology, on the other hand, is the child of evolution, reared under the tutelage of Cuvier and Lamarck, Von Baer and Haeckel, Darwin and Huxley, and taken into the service of comparative anatomy and embryology. It is a branch of philosophy dealing partly with positive data,

A partly also with fanciful abstractions culled from the contemplation of concrete phenomena, but quite distinct from the soul of mankind, although dependent for its existence upon the human understanding.

Human life is guarded and controlled by laws, the principles and spirit of which have been evolved out of chaos by the mind of man stimulated thereto by the necessities of the fundamental claims of property, of exogamy, and of fear. The existence of non-human and undomesticated organisms is governed by natural laws which regard not individuals except in so far as they are subservient to the needs of the race to which they belong. In civilisation the individual is sacred and inviolable, but in nature obviously at a discount.

The geological record, made up as it is of organic remains preserved in a more or less fragmentary condition, must always continue to be incomplete precisely in regard to those organisms about whose past history information would be peculiarly acceptable, namely, the softbodied animals; but imperfect though it be, it suffices to show, what the historical record of seven thousand years fails to prove, that there is a specific as well as an individual longevity; and that when the form manifested by a given species, the resultant of a particular combination of heritable characters, becomes antiquated and PURPORT OF LIFE 3 incapable of prolonging the struggle against the influences, whether aggressively hostile or relentlessly dominating, which possess it from within and from without, it must give place, by substitution, to a new combination represented by a new form, which may be an outsider or a scion of the old stock.

Perhaps it may be said without undue presumption that it is one of the vanities of the imagination to consider that everything exists for his special behoof. This is one of those pious beliefs which are common to men and dogs. One of the elementary truths revealed by biology is this: that whatever use man may make of his contemporaries, and however successful he may be in bending them to his will or in exterminating them, the fact remains that they are not here to do his bidding but to find their own sustenance, to secure their own safety, and to propagate their own kind. They have an objective existence guided by instincts of which the superficial reactions alone can be observed and named. Biology is based upon a detached investigation of the properties of living matter, and is thus distinguished from teleology which depends upon an anthropocentric interpretation of the organic environment, whereas mythology may be said to proceed from an anthropomorphic conception of the inorganic environment.

Anatomy, defined as the science of the structure of organised bodies, is usually comprehended in the three faculties of human anatomy, zoological anatomy (zoology), and vegetable anatomy (botany). Each of these primary disciplines introduces the student to several paths of learning, *e.g.,* topographical anatomy (anatomy *sensu stricto),* physiological anatomy (physiology or the treatment of structure in relation to function), histological anatomy (histology or microscopic anatomy), ontogenetic anatomy (embryology), and philosophical anatomy (morphology). These are what Owen (1866) called the ways of anatomy.

Histology, the anatomy of the constituent parts or tissues of organs, is investigated by microscopical and microchemical methods which were pioneered by Xavier Bichat whose work, "Anatomie ge'nerale appliquee a la Physiologie" (1801), preceded by more than a quarter of a century the enunciation of the cell-theory. This theory laid the foundation of a great part of modern biological research, and it is a significant circumstance that it was published in the decade which witnessed the death of Cuvier (1832). It teaches that the ultimate units of all the tissues of an organism consist of nucleated protoplasmic bodies, conventionally termed cells, which are derived by repeated cell-division from a primordial fertilised egg-cell; and it also forms the basis of the subdivision of the animal ECONOMIC ZOOLOGY 5 kingdom into protozoa or unicellular animals, and metazoa or multicellular animals.

Having now briefly defined the objects and the position of our enquiry, let us turn for a moment to consider it from the economic or *cut bono* standpoint. Economic zoology is to morphology what the industrial arts are to fine art — with a difference upon which it is not necessary to insist. Many of the aforesaid objects of enquiry are so rarely seen that their disappearance from the face of the earth would not produce any perceptible effect upon the economy or balance of nature. Most living things are popularly conceived to be of no use in the wild state; and their extermination, so long as they remain indomitable and refuse, as it were, to take the oath of allegiance to man, appears to be inseparable from the progress of

civilisation. In many cases their specific longevity seems to be approaching the end, in precisely the same manner as is the racial longevity of the primitive and fast vanishing races of mankind.

The Rev. Gregor Mendel, Abbot of Briinn, whose experiments in practical heredity are now appraised by some of his followers at an even higher rate than those of Charles Darwin, was coeval with his posthumous rival, though apparently unknown to him even by repute. They were contemporaries working independently along the same general lines though with different perspectives and methods, the one exercising a profound substantive influence upon his day and generation, and occasioning a great public disputation, the personal influence being permanent, the public disputation ending in platitudes; the other, in the quietude of the sanctuary, unseen and unknown except to a few intimates, pursuing far-reaching numerical researches which have been rescued from oblivion years after their good author had been laid to rest, secure alike from excommunication and from hair-splitting controversy. Students of practical questions of heredity confess to the hope that their investigations may lead to the regeneration not only of cultivated and domesticated races of plants and animals but also of the human race, by the selection and perpetuation of desirable characters and the weeding out of undesirables. From this point of view their work has undoubtedly a direct economic significance.

In the same way as benefiting humanity, the discoveries in protozoology and parasitology which have rendered the infancy of this century so illustrious, of the relations of protozoa to certain epidemic and epizootic diseases, the life-histories and nuclear changes of the parasites, and their transmission by intermediate hosts; as well as such discoveries as that of the conveyance of plague bacilli by rat-fleas, of the SUMMUM BON-UM 7 micrococci of Malta fever by goats, and Looss's discovery of the stereotropism or contact requirements of the larva of the tunnel worm *(Anchylostomum)* — all of these are of primary

hygienic importance.

So much however cannot be said convincingly of purely morphological researches. The origin of the human race, the ancestry of vertebrates, the correct systematic position of fleas, and other cognate problems perennially awaiting solution, are matters of no importance in domestic life, and it is hard to believe that they ever will possess any such value. Although it may be true that to the individual worker it is the *summum bonum* when his science overtakes a human need, it does not follow that we must accept the theory that every scientific fact will sooner or later directly and materially benefit mankind at large, and that this consideration should be the guiding motive of scientific investigation. Many precious facts have been For an account of a group of wingless Diptera to which fleas do not appear to be related except by convergence, and the amusing controversy to which it gave rise, the following papers may be consulted:— 1. F. Dahl, "Puliciphora, eine neue, flohahnliche Fliegengattung," *Zool. Anz.,* 1897, pp. 409-412; translated by E. E. Austen in *Ann. Nat. Hist,* (vii.) I. pp. 99-101, 1898 (Puliciphora, a new flea-like genus of Diptera.) 2. B. Wandolleck, "1st die Phylogenese der Aphanipteren entdeckt?" *Zool. Anz.,* 1898, pp. 180-182. 3. F. Dahl, " Ober Puliciphora lucifera," *Zool. Anz.,* 1898, p. 308. 4. B. Wandolleck, "Die Stethopathidae eine neue fliigel —und schwingerlose Familie der Diptera," *Zool. Jahrb. Syst.,* xi., 1898, pp. 412-441.

lost for ever in the cataclysms of the past without damaging the prospects of the human race. It is certain, however, that morphological researches, and the speculations which proceed from them, contribute to the precision of our rational conceptions, and on this account they cannot be neglected. Their intellectual value is an indication of their art. But I will not run the risk of sapping the strength of morphology by enquiring too closely where it lies.

Biometrical researches, using the expression in an extended sense to include all statistical studies of variation and cell-lineage, have, on the whole, as little in common with morphology as with parasitology. But the point of view of biologists undergoes periodical change, as indeed it must do, for unless the methods and the outlook are varied the art will be lost. The scope of any method is limited, more narrowly in some cases than in others; and after it has been tested by a crowd of workers its limitations become uncomfortably patent, and one turns with relief to something altogether new. At the same time it should be remembered that the application of what may be termed *ad hoc* methods to the elucidation of morphological problems may only serve to demonstrate the inadequacy of such methods in respect of that particular application. What yields good results in heredity may not be equally fruitful when TYPOLOGY 9 applied to phylogeny, the origin of the leading branches of the tree of life.

Morphology in general treats of the evolution of forms and organs within the compass of a given type. Phylogeny does this too, and more besides, since it is concerned with the almost impossible task of tracing the pedigrees of the primary types themselves. A little explanation may be necessary at this point to render my meaning intelligible. The word "type" has been used in many different senses, and is consequently a dangerous equivocal word to trifle with, though very convenient. Examples of types of the first order of magnitude are the platyhelminth type, the annelid type, the arthropod type, the molluscan type, the vertebrate type. Probably in consequence of a reaction against the old dogmatic use of the term, these types have, at one time or another, been connected together by imaginary links in a manner which in many cases, is now recognised as being quite inadmissible or, as we may otherwise express it, in a manner contrary to the canons of the art of morphology. Hopeless pictures and impossible pedigrees have resulted from this confusion of ideas. The criteria of homology are indeed hard to define, being partly intuitive, but we may find some indications which may assist towards their future formulation. The fish type,

the bird type, and the mammalian type may be quoted as instances of the second order of magnitude; the hoofed mammal or ungulate type and the primate type are of the third order; the odd-toed ungulate of the fourth order; the equine type and the human type are examples of the fifth order of magnitude. Lower categories are exemplified by the type genus of a family, the type species of a genus, and the type individual of a species, the last being purely conventional, referring to the actual specimen upon which the original specific description was based. The types of cultivated races are determined in a somewhat different manner.

From the fourth grade downwards it is frequently possible to determine the pedigree of a specialised type from a more generalised ancestry, with considerable probability of accuracy and, in some cases, as with the pig, horse, and elephant, with a great deal of precision. In the superior grades it becomes increasingly difficult to arrive at an understanding. It is something to be able to say that the vertebrate type can be traced with certainty to a chordate type; but it cannot be asserted without contradiction that the craniate vertebrate is derived from an acraniate chordate; because the gap between these two grades of organisation is too great, and many of the intervening stages of substitution and of cephalisation (head-formation) are lost.

ORGANIC SYMMETRY n

Phylogeny and heredity illustrate different phases of the theory of descent with modification, and have to be approached by appropriate methods. The test of breeding, which is crucial in heredity, is obviously inapplicable in a phylogenetic investigation where the last positive links in the chain of evidence can, as a rule, only be afforded, if at all, by palaeontology.

Morphology, in its aesthetic aspect, is the perception of symmetry and organic beauty. Its interest and importance lie less in its ultimate truth than in its relative completeness, by which I mean its capacity for embracing the widest possible range of facts without ignoring

those which may not fall into harmony with a particular theory.

The distinction between convergent and normal morphogeny has long pervaded biological litera_iuie_; but I believe it to be a fact that the equality of interest which attaches to the two branches of the subject has not been recognised in an adequate manner hitherto. It will appear in the course of this essay _that_ convergence is neither identical with homoplasy nor with cenojjenesis, but that it includes these and some Homoplasy signifies similarity; pf form unaccompanied_ by cpjprnunity of pedigree. As explained below, we owe the term to Sir Ray Lankester. Cenogenesis implies the origin of structural features by relatively recent adaptation, "in contrast"" witlljalingenesis or primordial adaptation. The terms are dueTo Professor Hasckel, thing else besides. All homoplasy is convergence, but all convergence is not homoplasy; and the same dictum may be repeated, *mutatis mutandis,* for cenogenesis. Professor H. F. Osborn, in the paper to which I have referred in the Preface, finds homoplasy to be of very great importance in the evolution of mammalian teeth, "because it seems to coincide with the principle of definite or determinate evolution" which has proceeded "independently in a great many different families of mammals." He discusses the special value of the evolution of teeth as bearing upon homoplastic mutations, inasmuch as teeth are preformed beneath the gum so that "new cusps, folds, crests, and styles are invariably congenital." CHAPTER II PHYSIOLOGICAL CLASSIFICATION

The animal kingdom, according to the teaching which was customary in Professor Huxley's time, was arranged under the two great divisions of the vertebrata or animals provided with a jointed axial skeleton, the backbone, and the invertebrata or animals destitute of a backbone; whereby a single phylum or primary branch of the tree of life was contrasted and placed upon an apparent equality with a whole complex of other phyla. This method of classification denoted one of the great generalisations in zoology at the birth of the nineteenth century, enduring from the beginning to the end of that century. Those who attend to these matters no longer continue to oppose the homogeneous group of the vertebrates to the negative association of invertebrates. The former term, introduced by Lamarck and Cuvier, retains its full significance, but the word invertebrate, though still useful as an adjective, is comparatively barren as an idea.

The classification now adopted is one based upon a profounder analysis of the animated frame, namely, upon the cellular constitution of the body. This second great generalisation, as we have seen above, had already been achieved during the first half of the preceding century, but the fate of the backbone in classification was not sealed until the end. In the light of recent researches we may find a further reason, besides the fallacy of contrasting non-equivalent groups, for discarding the older method. The presence of a backbone is a character which does not pair with the absence of one, but it does pair with the presence of a notochord.

We may venture to lay down, as a fundamental principle in morphology, that only those characters pair which are connected together by the bond of substitution. By way of extending this principle one step further whilst reference is being made to the vertebrata, we may add that the presence of a bony endoskeleton is a character which pairs morphologically with a cartilaginous endoskeleton, but not with a horny exoskeleton. On the other hand the vertebrate endoskeleton, in its capacity of affording attachment to muscles, can be compared physiologically with an arthropod exoskeleton or a molluscan shell.

A morphological classification must be physiologically true, *i.e.,* it must conform to physiological laws; but a physiological classification is DUAL CLASSIFICATION i under no corresponding obligation, and it is partly through losing sight of this circumstance of the differential purport of morphology and physiology, partly also through lack of knowledge of palaeozoic physiology, that much confusion has arisen.

Returning now to the consideration of the dual classification of the animal kingdom:—the current system, which has received so much additional stability by the recent progress of protozoology, recognises the two great subdivisions of the protozoa and the metazoa. It is sometimes considered an advantage to unite all unicellular organisms under the Haeckelian term protista from which are derived the parallel stems of the metazoa and the metaphyta (multicellular plants). In the vegetable kingdom the transition from unicellular to multicellular forms is graduated even amongst existing natural orders; and the algae include both kinds.

The protozoa are commonly treated as a phylum of the animal kingdom equivalent in classification to the other phyla, but this procedure is not in strict accordance with facts. The protozoa occupy a position which is unique, and they are rightly contrasted with the polyphyletic metazoa. There is no such abstraction as a protozoan type in the same sense as there is a molluscan type or a vertebrate type, because the combination of characters which is common to all protozoa is also that which is common to all metazoan cells, except their independence. The positive distinction between protozoa and metazoa is thus justified alike on morphological and on physiological grounds.

It remains to be seen whether there are not some other properties of animals that could be utilised temporarily for the purpose of obtaining a comprehensive survey, beyond those which are afforded by their bodily composition. A grouping of physiologically comparable forms may indeed be very instructive, and it has this additional advantage that it enables us to visualise, in a single perspective, a multitude of facts which would otherwise lie beyond our range for the time being. It will thus be seen that physiology can render great service in marshalling together scattered morphological units. In support of the soundness of these assertions I may quote the following statement from Prof. A. A. W. Hubrecht's recent monographic essay on the "Early Ontogenetic Phenomena in Mammals." Referring to the relation between trophoblast and amnion of which he is the exponent, he says:—

"A. Willey ('98) has speculated upon similar relations between arthropod embryos and their larval envelope, also designated as amnion, in *Quart. Journ. Micro. Sc,* vol. liii., 1908, p. 76. The trophoblast is the outer absorbent germlayer attached to the embryos of many viviparous animals.
LAND AND WATER 17 *Peripatus, Lepisma, Gryllus, Forficula,* and others; has rightly interpreted the direct comparability with the vertebrate trophoblast, and has looked upon it (as I have done '95 B for vertebrates) as an adaptation to a viviparous habit acquired by the terrestrial descendant of an aquatic ancestor."

An example of a simple and obvious physiological system of classification, based upon distribution and covering the entire animal kingdom, is that which distinguishes between aquatic and land animals. There is a peculiar propriety in this disposition inasmuch as all the groups of land animals have had a more or less remote aquatic ancestry, some inconceivably remote, others comparatively recent; whilst others again have reverted to an aqueous medium in which their lives are spent. Land mollusca, land leeches, land nemertines, land planarians, and land crabs, are examples of terrestrial groups which have had a recent aquatic ancestry, their immediate congeners being still aquatic animals.

The general structural differences which are associated with the radical change of environment are chiefly connected with the organs of respiration and, to a less extent, those of locomotion. In some cases, as with the operculate land molluscs, the change from water to land has only affected the organ of respiration. In others no striking alteration is manifested in essential organs, although accessory structures sometimes

B appear, as in *Birgus latro,* the coconut robber crab, where there is an accessory pulmonary chamber above the gills, and in *Ampullaria,* a tropical freshwater operculate snail living in tanks and swamps exposed to drought, where there is an analogous arrangement. An interesting and rather subtle change has taken place in the habits of typical land leeches in that they have lost the power of swimming, having become entirely stereotropic.

Purely aquatic creatures are those which breathe by absorbing the oxygen dissolved in the water, and they are sometimes called "waterbreathing" animals on that account. If kept in a limited volume of water the oxygen would become exhausted and the animals asphyxiated unless the water was frequently renewed as it is in an aquarium. Asphyxiation sometimes takes place under natural conditions in low-lying swamps when the water in the deeper places becomes stagnant after a prolonged drought. The mud-dwelling fishes at the bottom may then be seen swimming spasmodically towards the surface to gulp in atmospheric air, often too late to recover from the poisonous effect of the noxious gases below.

There are many partially or completely aquatic animals which find their food under water and *Birgus* and *Ampullaria* are figured in Scraper's " Animal Life," London, 1890.
AMPHIBIA 19 whose appendages are adapted for swimming, although they breathe atmospheric air and are therefore true air-breathers. The cetacea and the sirenia are completely aquatic in so far that if they are driven ashore by storm or accident they are irretrievably lost; at the same time they can only breathe air. The distinction between air-breathers and water-breathers is therefore more fundamental than that between aquatic and terrestrial animals. The intermediaries between these two groups are the amphibious creatures which are by no means confined to the class Batrachia or Amphibia *sensu stricto,* but include all land crabs, some molluscs, and even certain fishes, both dipnoan and teleostean, as well as some reptiles.

The essential organs which perform the principal functions of the body might each in turn be made the basis of a physiological classification which would convey a certain amount of information to those for whom such knowledge possesses any value. More interesting for our present purpose are such groupings as depend upon the relations of animals to their immediate surroundings irrespective of the actual nature of the environment, and it will be seen that the pairs of characters illustrated by the dual subdivisions which will be discussed below, virtually coincide in their nature with some of the primary differences between animals and plants.

The various tactics to which animals and plants resort when driven by necessity or threatened by danger, and the reactions which they exhibit towards external stimuli such as heat, light, drought, moisture, contact, proximity of food and of hostile influences, have long engaged the attention of biologists for the reason, amongst others, that the differently constituted nervous system of invertebrate animals and the lack of this system in plants, in protozoa, and in sponges, impart a special character to their vital reactions, in contrast with the more or less intelligent responses of craniate vertebrates. All the tendencies or "tropisms" to which protoplasm is liable are to be observed, either positively or negatively, in every organism, and frequently, at different times, both positively and negatively in the same species.

One of the most commonly observed reactions is that known as phototaxis or heliotropism, these terms being, however, not quite synonymous inasmuch as the reaction to sunlight (*i.e.,* heliotropism in the strict sense) is not the same *Cf.* J. von Uexkull, "Leitfaden in das Studium der experimentellen Biologie der Wassertiere." Wiesbaden, 1905.

M. Verworn, "Allgemeine Physiologie," 4th edit., Jena, 1903. English translation " General Physiology" from the 2nd edit. by F. S. Lee, London, 1899.

H. S. Jennings, "Behaviour of the Lower Organisms." New York, 1906.

J. E. Duerden, "On the Habits and Reactions of Crabs bearing Actinians in their Claws." *P. Zool. Soc* London, ii. 1905 (1906). ATTRACTION OF LIGHT 21 as that to artificial light (*i.e.,* phototaxis in the narrower sense). Professor Max Verworn, whose work on General Physiology has done so much to give precision to the interpretation of elementary vital phenomena, apparently wishes to discard the term heliotropism altogether in favour of phototaxis; but there are certain cases which oppose this blending of terms.

The nocturnal lepidoptera are negatively heliotropic but positively phototactic, being impelled by an irresistible attraction to a bright lamp. Amphioxus, the lancelet, is passively heliotropic, but actively phototactic, evincing extreme agitation upon the approach of a lighted candle at night. In the same way fishes are attracted by torchlight at sea, and lighted lamps are placed at the head of fish-traps, where they are kept burning all night to attract prawns which are required for bait in large quantities. Lighted prawn-traps and moth-traps represent practical applications of the knowledge of the phototactic properties of these animals. The phosphorescent organs of deep-sea fishes no doubt also act as luminous lures.

An intimate acquaintance with the habits and reactions of animals is not confined to the human race. Many reptiles, birds, and mammals are accomplished field entomologists, knowing where to look for their food, and how to distinguish edible from inedible kinds. The tropical tree lizard *Calotes* will take its stand beside a beehive to catch the bees as they issue, swallowing them entire; or beside an incipient termite mound picking off the workers. Bulbuls will gather round a swarming termite nest and decimate the winged emigrants. Bats will fly to a bright light, not because they are themselves attracted by it, but because they know where to find insects, especially winged termites, which are. Geckoes and toads similarly approach artificial light in search of insect food. In the three last-mentioned examples of nocturnal animals seeking their food by artificial light we find once more (as in the case of moths) positive phototaxis in apparent conflict with negative heliotropism.

It seems important to take notice of this association of contrary reflexes, of which more instances will be found below. Meanwhile it may be useful to distinguish habits from reactions:—a habit is the behaviour of an animal in the open; a reaction is its behaviour in the laboratory. Finally, whilst dealing with definitions we may add that the word tropism means the tendency to react in a definite manner towards external stimuli.

Mr Francis Buckland has recorded a similar observation of the common toad eating bees in Oxfordshire. CHAPTER III EXPOSED AND CONCEALED ANIMALS (PHANEROZOA AND CRYPTOZOA)

Phanerozoic or diurnal animals are positively heliotropic; cryptozoic animals including crepuscular, nocturnal, and subterranean forms, in fact all that avoid the light of day, are negatively heliotropic. Flights of butterflies at high noon are followed by swarms of hawkmoths and noctuids at twilight. The contrast is particularly well illustrated on a broad and spectacular scale by the interchange of amenities between such gregarious creatures as crows and the so-called flying foxes or fruit-eating bats, due to their homing in the same place, as may be observed daily in certain favourable localities in the maritime districts of Ceylon. I recorded these facts in "Spolia Zeylanica," after mentioning them in a letter to the late Professor Alfred Newton who expressed his appreciation of them. These animals keep remarkably regular hours of work and sleep, the birds foraging by day, the bats by night.

At one place in particular, a small lighthouse islet off the south-west coast named Barberyn, which is covered by a coconut plantation, they congregate in the palm trees alternately by night and by day. If one crosses over to the island in the heat of the day all is quiet and nothing out of the common is to be noted; but about the time of sunset a great commotion of crows among the tree tops bursts upon the ear, and gradually subsides in the dusk of the evening. This signalises the arrival home of the colony of crows after their day's work is over. The approach of sunrise, on the other hand, is announced by the chattering and squabbling of numerous flying foxes overhead.

At sundown the passage of immense flocks of crows and flying foxes in opposite directions across the strait which divides the island from the mainland can be witnessed, the former bound for the island to rest for the night, the latter speeding their way to the mainland intent upon their nocturnal forage. The flying foxes travel on the average distinctly higher than the crows, starting singly and increasing to large flocks of twenty-five and upwards, finally becoming a continuous stream. The crows obviously outnumber the bats, although weight for weight they probably represent an equiva The grey-necked Indian crow, *Corvus splendens Pteropus medius.* CROWS AND FLYING FOXES 35 lent bulk of living matter. In the evening the crows begin to arrive in small numbers before the vanguard of the bats has started, increasing in their turn to large battalions until a period of maximum migration is reached, and then troops of bats are to be seen passing over still larger columns of crows in the opposite direction, the whole of the cross-migration occupying about half an hour. The reverse passage, namely, the matutinal flight, takes place towards sunrise, the bats returning from the mainland to rest for the day suspended in rows from the midribs of the palm leaves, the crows crossing over on their daily quest for garbage. This instance may be classed as one of convergent homing, the same trees affording hospitality in regular alternation to day-flying birds and night-flying mammals.

Phanerozoa and cryptozoa are two well-marked physiological groups, comprising between them all the forms of animal life; and the distinction is paralleled by the following more fundamental contrast between animals and plants. In general habit and mechanism of growth the vegetable kingdom as a whole exhibits positive phototaxis in the wide sense, whereas the animal kingdom as a whole seems to show negative phototaxis; the former proposition can be accepted without question, but the latter requires substantiation. Passing over the vast array of strictly cryptozoic forms, it may be noted in the first place that while the green colouring matter of plants effects its characteristic reaction, the chlorophyll reaction, by reason of its exposure to sunlight, the respiratory pigments of animals which promote another kind of gaseous interchange, are enclosed in blood-vessels and sinuses, generally concealed from the light by an opaque skin, and always independent of the light, even though the skin should happen to be transparent.

As a second example to illustrate broadly the essential cryptotaxis (tendency to concealment) of animals, may be mentioned the well-known fact that even among the higher vertebrates many birds and most mammals are, in the wild state, concealed from view by their protective coloration. Of course this does not in itself shelter them from the sun; the environment provides the cover; but it protects them from the visual acuity of their enemies, many of which are notoriously cryptotactic. A common method of shooting wild animals, for sport or for food, is to lie in wait at night concealed behind an ambush within range of a water-hole where they will come to drink. The largest mammals, whether carnivorous or herbivorous, such as the tiger, elephant, and giraffe, are known to be almost invisible when at rest in the forest, jungle, and high grass which they frequent in the daytime. In Ceylon, the rounded CHROMATISM 27 bosses of gneiss with their dark smoothly weathered surfaces, which are such prominent features in the landscape in many parts of the country, often present an uncommon resemblance to the form of the elephant; and the converse is equally true as may be verified when a herd of elephants is seen against a background of gneiss, the likeness being based upon the possession of a common ground colour superimposed upon a ponderous bulk.

Gorgeously coloured butterflies and beetles, small flower-haunting birds, such as the hummingbirds of the New World and the sun-birds of the Old World, whose plumage reflects a wonderful metallic lustre, larger birds with majestic males, the powerful diurnal birds of prey, and others afford, to the general rule of concealment, exceptions which do not stultify the rule but are explicable on special grounds of adaptation, selection, season, locality, and dominance.

Butterflies exhibit themselves in their seasonal flights sometimes in vast numbers, but their abundance at certain times only serves to accentuate their absence or rarity at others; the rapidity with which an immense noon-day swarm can efface itself is marvellous to behold; while the pupae and even the larvae are often quite concealed by various devices of shape, position, and colour. So with diurnal birds, the nests of the commonest are often very hard to find and rarely seen.

Land planarians offer instances of cryptozoic animals which are brightly coloured; the species are differentiated according to their colour markings, and richly tinted individuals are to be found in rotten logs in a dormant state by day, with the body looped in a characteristic manner; if left unobserved for a short time exposed to light, they glide rapidly away to a place of concealment.

A journey through any tropical forest or jungle, or even a little reflection will, I think, suffice to convince one that while the vegetation is luxuriantly phanerotactic, animal life is predominantly cryptotactic. The jungle is like the desert and the ocean, to all superficial appearances frequently devoid of animal life. This is possibly not the impression which one would receive from the perusal of faunistic works; but it is certainly that which is produced by observations in the open, and I regard it as one of the radical bionomical or habitual differences between animals and plants.

Vegetation is always exposed, it is permanently phanerotactic, but the most conspicuous animals in the natural state are only partially or periodically so. In many instances, especially among the hoofed mammals (Ungulata), the cryptotaxis can be properly appreciated only under natural conditions. Arboreal mammals, such as squirrels and monkeys, are amongst the most clearly phanerotactic members of the class Mammalia, but DAY AND NIGHT 29 many of the arboreal Lemurs, the most primitive of the order Primates, are strictly nocturnal and hence cryptotactic. Burrowing mammals are generally nocturnal as well, including the egglaying mammals of Australia, the scaly ant-eaters, ground-porcupines, and others too numerous to mention; the combination of fossorial with diurnal habits is rare, the common rabbit affording an instance of it. Others resort during the daytime to ready-made holes, hollow trees and caves, as the dasyures, mungooses, and sloth-bears. Some species exhibit mixed habits; but the cryptotactic tendency is universal amongst mammals.

It is not possible to tabulate lists of phanerozoa and cryptozoa, because all animals have cryptozoic potentialities. Those that are not definitely cryptotactic have the power of retreating to cover at the sign of danger; or of causing the aggressor to vanish from the scene by reason of their weapons of offence. The scent-glands of the mephitic skunk, of the naked bat *(Chiromeles)*, and in a lesser degree of the civet cats, are cryptotactic organs of a virulent type notwithstanding that they effect their object through the olfactory sense; besides being protected by their secretions, these animals are nocturnal. Scorpions, centipedes, and poisonous snakes are cryptozoic as well as armed for attack, so that they also are doubly protected and doubly dreaded by their enemies.

A special example of the cryptozoic tendency in poisonous snakes is the behaviour of the cobra in captivity in the presence of its food. Many Eastern jugglers and gipsies carry cobras about with them coiled up in round flat baskets, which are kept covered except during a performance. These cobras are fed upon eggs, which they swallow whole without breaking the shell. If they are preparing to cast their skin, and the eyes are glazed, they do not take food. But if they are in a normally hungry condition they will not touch a proffered *egg* so long as the basket is uncovered. If the cover is removed again two or three minutes after it has been replaced with the *egg* in the basket, the *egg* will be found to have been swallowed, and can be perceived travelling down the gullet by the protuberance which it causes; a second *egg* may be taken in like manner shortly afterwards.

Mr Frank Buckland ("Curiosities of Natural History," second series, reprinted, London 1903, p. 131) wanted to see whether a hedgehog would eat a common harmless snake. He caught a snake near Harrow, and bought a hedgehog in St Giles's. For several mornings he placed them together on the grass; but they took no notice of each other. At last, one evening, he shut them both up in a box together. During the night the hedgehog attacked and devoured half the snake, beginning at the tail. In a PHOTOPHOBIA 31 few more hours the rest of the snake was consumed.

Blood-sucking leeches prefer to feed under cover and, when gorged, retreat to cover as quickly as may be. A Ceylon land leech which I was keeping under observation remained on my arm for ten minutes without attempting to puncture the skin, in a contracted, flushed, quiescent posture. I then placed a silk handkerchief over the waiting worm, with the result that two minutes later a puncture was felt, and the attachment continued for thirty-eight minutes. When the leech was placed upon a dead leaf after the meal it immediately crawled underneath.

Apart from parasitism, the purest expression of cryptotaxis is that which is manifested by genuine cave-dwellers, and by animals which not only burrow underground, but also find their food underground, such as the mole-crickets *Gryllotalpa)*, the earthworms and the creatures which feed upon them, namely, moles, worm-eating slugs *(Testacel-*

la), earth-snakes *Uropeltidce),* and apodous Batrachia *(Caciliidce).* I have kept an *Ichthyophis* alive for ten months in one half of a coconut shell covered over by the other half, feeding it exclusively upon earthworms.

The most primitive members of the phylum Arthropoda are to a great extent cryptozoic; in Ceylon there is a species of the Thysanuran *Gryllotalpa* flies to artificial light.

genus *Machilis* which is found living on the moist and shaded surfaces of lichen-covered treetrunks and rocks, the mottled appearance of which the insects closely resemble. It is doubtless in virtue of this singular property of concealment that so many of the primitive forms have survived to the present day to be at once the delight and bewilderment of the systematise The noxious arthropods, which are only too familiar in certain quarters, are also cryptozoic, but it may be satisfactory to note that they are not primitive, they belong irreclaimably to the things of darkness.

Earthworms are well known to every horticulturist and tiller of the soil, and to every one who has read Darwin's famous book about them, but the other cryptozoa *(sensu stncto)* are hardly known outside the ranks of specialists. Darwin estimated that in many parts of England more than ten tons of dry earth annually passes through the bodies of earthworms on each acre of land. Equally impressive figures could be given to show the amount of sand-casting performed by the lug worms *(Arenicolidat)* on some temperate shores, and by the Enteropneusta *(Balanoglossus)* on some tropical shores.

So far I have referred almost exclusively to land animals because they are most in evidence by the effects which they produce in relation to husbandry. Predatory aquatic animals, especially CRYPTOTAXIS 33 the marine mammals, sea snakes, the larger fishes, free-swimming molluscs and Crustacea *e.g.,* Portunidae, the swimming crabs), may be described as phanerozoic; but we may confidently assert that in all cases a definite cryptotactic bias of varying intensity could be demonstrated. The large

Cephalopod molluscs, including the squids, cuttlefishes, and octopus, actually have a cryptotactic mechanism, the ink-sac, by the compression of which a black fluid is discharged, effectually covering the retreat of the individuals.

Nautilus, with its great external chambered shell, has no ink-sac, but lives in deep water and presents a scheme of pigmentation which secures its partial invisibility; the upper part of the body has the form of a fleshy hood from the dark-brown surface of which arise whitish, wart-like prominences giving a mottled coloration to the exposed part of the body, which harmonises well with the zebra-like markings on the shell. These simulate the play of light upon the surface ripples of the sea, whence I called them "ripple-markings. " On one occasion I accidentally dropped a healthy Nautilus overboard in four or five fathoms of very clear water in Sandal Bay, Lifu (Loyalty Islands), and, notwithstanding the translucency of the water, it disappeared instantaneously from view, and baffled all the efforts of an expert native diver, who was with me on the raft, to recover it, the alternate c light and dark bands on the shell constituting a most effective cryptic device.

The multitudes of floating organisms which compose what is known as the plankton, the primary food-supply of sea, river, and lake, are often rendered invisible by their extreme transparency. The animals which feed upon them do not pursue them by the aid of sight, but simply engulf them. Conversely, many of them have what may be called a phanerotactic mechanism, rendering them phosphorescent and visible at night. The utility of this mechanism to the owners of it is not very clear; it may be a product of metabolism, neither useful nor dangerous.

The basic quality underlying all animal life is the cryptic, the fear of the sun. Basking in the sun is a dangerous pastime.

CHAPTER IV

Free And Fixed Animals (eleutherozoa And Statozoa)

We may now consider briefly another

couple of essential properties of plants and animals, and note once more how the contrasted qualities are paralleled within the limits of the animal kingdom alone. The power of automatic locomotion, of executing free movements of translation from place to place, is one of the distinctive privileges of animals. The property of becoming rooted to the soil, and of undergoing perennial growth and regeneration, is the no less picturesque attribute of plants.

So inseparable from animal life did mobility appear, that the sponges, hydroids, corals, and bryozoa were formerly classed together as zoophytes, and were either believed to be plants of a peculiar kind or, as the name implies, to partake of the nature of both plants and animals. The purely animal nature of the coral polyps was established in the middle of the eighteenth century, that of sponges towards the middle of the nineteenth. Sponges were distinguished from the other zoophytes by the absence of polyps, but at an early stage of modern investigation the discovery was made that currents of water enter the body of the sponge through small pores in its outer wall, and leave it through larger apertures called oscula; subsequently the free-swimming ciliated larva was made known. In the same way the structure and life-history of other fixed or sessile animals were described, and it became an axiom that all such animals have been derived from free-living ancestors.

True sessile animals have been defined as those which, during the greater portion of their lives, are unable to transport themselves from the spot to which they have become attached, but, unlike parasites, are able to secure their own sustenance. Each phylum, with the exception of the craniate Vertebrata, has sedentary members; all sponges, most actinians (corals and sea anemones), and hydroids are sessile; comparatively few echinoderms are fixed at the present age, but "the combined evidence of comparative anatomy, embryology, and palaeontology indicates that the Echinoderma owe most of their obvious characters... to their having passed through a pelmatozoic (stalked) stage, *i.e.,* a stage in which the animal was attached by a part of its body wall." The recent and F. A. Bather, "Echinoderma in Lankester's Treatise on Zoology," part iii., 1900, p. 3.

SEDENTARY HABITS 37 extinct echinoderms are accordingly divided into two grades: A. Pelmatozoa; B. Eleutherozoa *(s. sir.).*

The remarkable prevalence of the sedentaryhabit amongst the lower *i.e.* invertebrate) animals seems to indicate that something peculiarly primordial lies at the back of the phenomenon, and makes it desirable that it should be expressed in physiological classification. I venture to assume the liberty to employ two contrasting terms in a wide physiological sense, which have been used already in a narrow morphological sense, namely, Eleutherozoa or free animals, and Statozoa or sedentary animals.

The effects of the sedentary habit upon the growth and organisation of the animals accustomed to it have been amply discussed by Semper, Lang, and others, and need not be described here; but it would be instructive if we could establish the existence of a primary function which formed the physiological basis of all this varied fixation occurring in widely separated morphological groups. There is an extra value in this inasmuch as we might by its means obtain some light upon a number of perplexing problems to which no direct answer is possible, *e.g.,* as to whether the fixed hydroidphase is more primitive than the free medusoidphase in Hydromedusae; or again as to whether In morphological nomenclature Statozoa is synonymous with Pelmatozoa *(vide* Bather, *op. cit.)* the free Appendicularise (tailed, pelagic Ascidians or Tunicata) are to be derived from fixed or from free-swimming ancestors. These questions may be resolved into one, that of the statozoic origin of Medusae and Appendiculariae respectively. Analogy affords no safe guide in solving such a riddle as this. There must be some common principle lying at the root of such a widely spread phenomenon as that of the fixation of animals; and in my judg-

ment the principle is expressed in the term stereotropism invented by J. Loeb.

As a typical example of the positive working of the stereotropic reaction Loeb quotes Dewitz's account (1885-1886) of the fertilisation of the *egg* of the cockroach. The spermatozoa are attracted by any surface; when examined in a drop of salt solution under the microscope they are seen to be adhering to the slide and coverglass, none being free in the middle of the drop. If a glass bead is introduced into the drop they adhere to that, never leaving it. "When once on the surface of the *egg,* the spermatozoa can no more leave it, but must move on its surface incessantly. In this way one spermatozoon finally reaches the micropyle and gets into the *egg.* The impregnation of the *egg* is therefore in Jacques Loeb, " Dynamics of Living Matter," New York, 1906, p. 156. Stereotropism implies contact requirements or the reaction to hard surfaces, STEREOTROPISM 39 this case a function of the stereotropism of the spermatozoa. " Loeb., *loc. citJ.*

As an instance of the negative working of the same reaction, Loeb quotes the case of the nauplii of *Balanus.* This does not appear to be so successful; it means either very little, or something which I do not understand. Referring to positive stereotropism, which I regard as a factor of great potentiality, Loeb explains that it is no real tropism inasmuch as lines of force do not exist. Much less then must negative stereotropism be responsive to force of any description; not only is it a negative quality, it is, as we shall see, practically nothing beyond words.

The acorn barnacles (Balanidae) make up the familiar crowded communities of white shelly bodies which are firmly attached to rocks between tide marks, and to other suitable surfaces. All barnacles are fixed, but these are doubly statozoic, cemented by their flat base without a stalk, in contrast with the goose barnacles (Lepadidae, pedunculate Cirripedes) which hang by a stalk attached to logs and other floating objects, sometimes to fishes, sea snakes, sea birds, and Crustacea.

The stalked barnacles, although fixed, chiefly affect what may be termed a planozoic (vagrant) habit analogous, up to a certain point, with that of ectoparasites. Commonly associated with floating communities of *Lepas,* are two planozoic Annelid worms, both belonging to the family Amphinomidse, *Hippono'e gaudichaudi* and *Amphinome rostrata.* The former is sometimes found between the valves of *Lepas* and is coloured pinkish orange like the *egg* ribbons of the barnacle. This association of forms has been met with on the Atlantic coast of North America, and I. have obtained them from the coast of Ceylon. Other planozoic forms with similar distribution associated with Sargassum or Gulf weed are the prawn *Leander natator* Bate, and the mollusc, *Scyllasa pelagica,* both of which simulate the colour and foliations of the brown seaweed upon which they live.

Lepas is specially interesting, as it combines the statozoic with the planozoic habit. As mentioned above, statozoic adults usually have free-swimming or pelagic, *i.e.,* pleotropic larvae, and the nauplius larva of barnacles, at least in its last phase when it is called the metanauplius, already possesses the primordium of the static mechanism, namely, the cement organs in the antennules. Therefore unless there is some special manifestation which Professor Loeb does not explain, it would seem desirable to describe the nauplius larvae as positively pleotropic, or J. P. Moore, "Some Pelagic Polychseta new to the Wood's Hole Fauna," *P. Ac Philad.,* vol. lv. part iii., 1903 (1904), pp. 793-Soi. *Cf.* "Korschelt und Heider. Lehrb. d. vergl. Entwicklungsgeschichte der wirbellose Thiere," Jena, 1890, p. 405. simply pelagic, rather than as negatively stereotropic. On the contrary, it is the intrinsic and latent stereotropism of the larvae which leads to the statozoic habit of the adult.

Furthermore the nauplii of Cirripedes are well known to be markedly heliotropic, and this character might temporarily mask their potential stereotropism, leading them out into the open sea. Groom obtained them in large numbers in the tow-net at Plymouth during February and March, 1893, belonging to a species which lives on the lime-stone rocks below the laboratory, in places considerably above high-tide mark, where they can only be moistened by the passing foam; but he was unable to rear them in confinement.

The Gastropod mollusca (snails, slugs, limpets), with their creeping adhesive foot, are pre-eminently stereotropic; yet it is not doubted that the typically pelagic or pleotropic Heteropoda and Pteropoda have been derived from them along different lines of descent. The free-swimming veliger larva of mollusca might be described equally well with the nauplius of *Balanus,* as showing negative stereotropism, and as indicating a free-swimming ancestry. It seems more just to suppose however that larvae i.T. T. Groom. "On the Early Development of Cirripedes." *Phil. Trans.,* London, vol. clxxxv., 1894, pp. 119-232. 2. A. Gruvel, "Monographic des Cirrhipedes," Paris, 1905, p. 445.

in general can be regarded with greater propriety as the vehicles of future adult types than as recapitulations of past ancestors. The larva, looked at synthetically in its entirety as an independent organism, apart from structural details, is essentially the vehicle of the adult, not that of an ancestral form. Thus the frog doubtless had a fish-like ancestor, but the tadpole, which is the fish-like larva of the frog, does not recapitulate the fish-like ancestor of the frog. The external facies of the tadpole is common to the larval or postlarval stages of many fishes, and represents a fundamental form likely to recur by convergence.

The oft-quoted Pilidium larva of Nemertine worms is an actual vehicle within human experience, a vehicle from which the worm alights when it has reached a certain stage on its journey through life. The Tornaria larva of Enteropneusta and the larval forms of Echinoderms which are related to it are also obviously nothing else but larval, *i.e.,* not ancestral forms in themselves. We may therefore repeat our dictum

that the nature of larval forms is that of vehicles of the future rather than relics of the past, true larval characters never having been adult characters.

For a recent discussion of the theory of recapitulation *see* the following: Adam Sedgwick, "The Influence of Darwin on the Study of Animal Embryology" in " Darwin and Modern Science," Cambridge, 1909.

It is sometimes customary to speak simply of positive and negative reactions, but it should not be forgotten that there are all degrees of stereotropism, from an occasional or facultative manifestation to a chronic condition, leading on to a definite sedentary habit. Many cases amongst the Annelid worms could be instanced where stereotropism and pleotropism (the free swimming habit) exist side by side, the latter frequently only manifesting itself at the breeding or swarming season, as with epigamous Nereids and the celebrated Palolo worm (Eunicidae) of Samoa and elsewhere in the South Seas.

Professor Hugo Eisig has made exact observations upon a number of Annelida Polychaeta, representing ten families, some of which exhibit a high degree of stereotropism together with an equally high degree of pleotropism, *e. g., Lepidasthenia* and *Ophiodromus.* Others again like *Psammolyce* and *Diopatra,* never advance beyond what is described as a swimming gait, *i.e.,* crawling along the bottom with a horizontal undulating movement of the body producing alternate arcs or waves of progression. When the amplitude of these undulations surpasses a certain magnitude, the rapidity of movement is thereby increased to such an extent that the animal rises from the bottom and swims through the water. It is a H. Eisig, *Ichthyotomussanguinarius.* Monograph 28 in "Fauna und Flora des Golfes von Neapel," Berlin, 1906, *see* pp. 190-297.

remarkable and suggestive fact that the typically pelagic Alciopidae, freed entirely from their stereotropic bonds, are usually very poor swimmers.

The case of *Nephthys* is worthy of special mention. This is one of the best

swimmers known amongst Annelids, although when left alone it passes most of its existence buried in the sand. Eisig found that, unlike *Psammolyce* which paddles along the bottom but never swims, *Nephthys* on the contrary undulates rapidly through the water, but never creeps along the bottom; it is either at rest or swimming, passing abruptly from the one condition to the other without an intervening reptant phase.

An analogous instance of spasmodic pleotropism on the part of a normally stereotropic and partly statozoic organism is the case of the bivalve mollusc, *Pecten* the scallop. "If disturbed the attached scallop can break or cast off its byssal threads and swim by clapping the shell"; the gaping ventral lips of the shell being directed forwards in locomotion.

The fact, elucidated by Dr Eisig, that the posture of the Annelid appendages or podia on opposite sides of the arcs is the same when the worm is progressing slowly along the bottom as when swimming rapidly through the water, has led him to the conclusion that the stereotropic movement (on the bottom) is secondary *Cf.* W. J. Dakin, "Memoir on Pecten," L.M.B.C. Memoir XVII., Liverpool, 1909.

LEECHES 45 as compared with the pleotropic movement (through the water), and is derived by inheritance from swimmers.

In the same strain, referring to Amphioxus, Dr Eisig *(loc. cit.,* p. 276) says that however primitive one may hold its organisation to be, yet nobody will assert that its limbless body and its predominantly cryptoid locomotion represent archaic features. I am unable to follow these conclusions myself, as I approach this matter independently from a cryptozoic and stereotropic standpoint; and in this, as in many another affair, everything depends upon the point of view. The facts are undeniable, but the way of dealing with them cannot be other than arbitrary.

Another instructive example of the association of stereotropism of a highly specialised type with well-marked pleotropism is afforded by some leeches. The stereotropism of the medicinal leech is of such a nature that it has passed into a proverb. Closely connected with this habit is its method of obtaining its food by sucking the blood of vertebrates. It progresses along a hard surface by the looping gait, and can also swim rapidly by vertical undulations of the body. The land leeches of Ceylon and Japan belong to genus *Hcemadipsa.* They also, as mentioned above, feed upon the blood of vertebrates, for which they exhibit a remarkable propensity which might almost be raised to the rank of a tropism. Professor C. O. Whitman has published observations on the Japanese land leech, some of which I have confirmed for the Ceylon land-leech, including the fact that it cannot swim; it is entirely stereotropic. It has the power of repairing or closing severe wounds, but cannot regenerate the head or the posterior sucker. The lack of the capacity for regeneration in leeches is paralleled by the similar behaviour of Amphioxus. Leeches offer as strong a contrast to other Annelids in this respect as Amphioxus does to the Enteropneusta.

The loss of the posterior sucker puts an end to the looping gait but not to the effort to achieve it, and the lack of adhesion behind is compensated by peristalsis on a level surface, and by the great power of extension possessed by the forebody when climbing up a vertical surface. On placing two leeches on a stone in the middle of a large dish of water they remained motionless in a sub-erect attitude, resting upon the hind-sucker for some time, and then descended into the water, looping along the bottom to the side of the vessel. When watching them by candle-light they would not venture across until the light was removed.

Quoted in the *Cambridge Natural History,* vol. ii., 1896, "Earthworms and Leeches," by F. E. Beddard, p. 408.

CEYLON LAND LEECH 47

Whilst sucking, abundant watery fluid issues from the epidermal glands of the Ceylon land leech, so copious that it may flow off the arm, upon which it happens to be feeding, like water. The glands occur on epidermal papillae which are retractile, and can be protruded simultaneously like a flush passing over the body. No spilling of blood takes place normally; but if some be taken and mounted in a drop of the epidermal fluid, the red corpuscles become aggregated together to form the characteristic rouleaux, whilst retaining their shape and healthy appearance. The fluid is perfectly clear, like the aqueous humour of the vertebrate eye, and forms an excellent medium for the examination of fresh blood.

In the Japanese land leech a similar fluid is stated to issue from the nephridial pores. I have not seen this in Ceylon; but when a feeding leech is turgid with blood, the nephridiopores become clearly visible, fourteen pairs situated in the lower half of the lateral pale bands at the posterior borders of the segments, the space of five annuli intervening between successive pores. There are three segments or fifteen annuli in front of the first pore; the posterior, nuchal eyes appear to lie on the second annulus. The erectile papillae are arranged in a single row across each annulus. Certain of these papillae have a special character and occur in longitudinal rows, lying singly in the first annulus of each segment *(i.e.,* in the annulus following that which carries the segmental nephridiopores); each shows a dark centre surrounded by a pale border on the top of a retractile papilla. These segmental ocelliform organs commence in the segment in front of the first nephridiopore, and there are twelve of them in each segment, *i.e.,* six on each side disposed as follows: two lateral rows, one above and one below the lateral band, a dorsolateral and a ventro-lateral row, a submedian dorsal and a submedian ventral row.

The preceding notes serve to illustrate, in respect of external characters alone, the highly specialised organisation of the land leech, which is already indicated by the concentration of its stereotropic mechanism, by its lack of regeneration, and by its passion for blood which amounts to a haematotropism, as no one can doubt who has read Sir Emerson Tennent's account of it, or who has experienced it in the flesh. Hardly anything proclaims a finished organisation, the culmination of a phyletic career, so plainly as an exclusive diet. In point of fact the leeches represent the culmination at the present age of the Annelid branch in a definite direction. Branches of the tree of life often terminate in a brush of points, not necessarily in a single point; and leeches constitute one of these terminations.

TREE SNAKES 49

Few free-living animals except terrestrial snakes, are so exquisitely stereotropic as are leeches; and snakes offer a further analogy with Annelids as a whole in the combination of stereotropism and pleotropism in some freshwater species, stereotropism alone in burrowing and in arboreal species, pleotropism alone in many marine species. In some tree snakes, *e.g., Dendrophis, Dendrelaphis,* and *Chrysopelea,* there is a lateral keel or suture on each side of the ventral shields. It has been suggested by Mr R. Shelford that this carination or hinging 01 the ventral shields, by allowing the body to flatten itself out and become concave below, enables the snake, when springing from a height, to descend gently like a parachute. Against this it has to be noted that burrowing snakes like *Cylindrophis,* which have very small ventral shields, are able to flatten the body in a marvellous manner. I rather think that the lateral hinge-lines are in the first instance an accessory stereotropic contrivance enabling the snakes to climb up rough tree-trunks with greater facility; moreover, a lateral angulation of the ventral shields is found in the terrestrial genera, *Lycodon* and *Hydrophobus.* Nevertheless, the possibility is not excluded that they might also serve on occasion for the parachute flight; but R. Shelford. A note on "Flying" Snakes, *P. Zool. Soc,* London, 1906, i., pp. 227-230.

D that the latter ever really takes place is a matter which requires confirmation.

Other reptiles which take refuge in trees, *e.g., Calotes* and *Varanus,* when alarmed, will project themselves from a great height to the ground without elaborating a mechanism for aerial flight. The case of *Draco,* the flying lizard of Malaya, where such a mechanism is developed (dermal membrane supported by ribs), belongs to a different category; and the facts seem to show clearly that it is not merely the habit of taking flying leaps, like monkeys, for example, that has led to the formation of organs of flight.

We may now submit the conclusion that just as all divisions of the animal kingdom display a cryptozoic bias, so do they all show a statozoic tendency. The sedentary habit is referable to a stereotropic basis, and pelagic or pleotropic forms belonging to groups which are predominantly sedentary, have had a probable statozoic origin. All land animals have had aquatic ancestors, or, more precisely, all air-breathers have descended from water-breathers as defined above. The latter are primarily aquatic, and are either stereotropic at the present time, or it may be argued that they have had a more or less remote stereotropic ancestry.

Thus the permanent fixation of so many aquatic animals is not such a bizarre phenomenon as it appeared to be to the older naturalists COMMON PROPERTIES 51 of the eighteenth century, but it is merely an extreme manifestation of a very primitive property of animal life. My coupling of the cryptozoic habit with the stereotropic reaction is incidentally justified by a statement of Eisig to the effect that stereotropism signifies rest and concealment. The purpose of this and the preceding chapter has been to insist upon the fundamental nature of cryptotaxis and stereotropism in the convergent evolution of animals. These are some of the primary properties of living matter upon which the moulding forces of nature have been at work for untold ages.

A somewhat analogous case, in so far as it is an extreme manifestation of a common property, is the electric power of the three typical kinds of electric fishes (ray, eel of South American rivers, and catfish of African rivers). As

shown by E. du Bois-Reymond, these fishes owe their capacity for imparting severe shocks, in different directions, to an intensification of the common electromotive properties of nerve and muscle. In each case, as pointed out by Dr D. S. Jordan, closely-related species show no trace of the electric endowment.

See " Biological Memoirs," Oxford, 1887, vol. i. "Guide to the Study of Fishes," 1905. CHAPTER V MIMICRY AND HOMOPLASY _the term convergence is applied to resemblances amongst animals which are not due to dirgct relationship or genetic affinity in other words, which are not derived by inheritance from common ancestors, but which result from independent functional adaptation to similar ends: *e.g.* , the exuviation and regeneration of newts as compared with the same phenomena in crabs and lobsters, or again the coiled prehensile tail and great rolling eyes, moving independently, of *Hippocampus* and Chameleons.

It has long been recognised as a dominant factor in comparative morphogeny. Common characters of adaptation in different.-animals may be due to common inheritaneer orthey may be due to convergence. Hence it follows, in Semper's words, that the problem of the morphologist is to learn to distinguish such These two striking instances of double convergence were presented in respective juxtaposition by Mr Frank Buckland. ("Curiosities of Natural History." Reprinted 1903, Macmillan, First and Second Series.) Compare the case of the egg-laying, duck-billed Platypus of Australia.

1 WAYS OF CONVERGENCE S3 characters as have been developed by adaptation, quite independently of the affinities of animals, from such as have been transmitted by inheritance through a long series of generations.

Morphology therefore naturally falls into two divisions: convergent morphogeny and homogenetic or normal morphogeny. The former is not generally admitted as a legitimate branch of positive morphology; the latter is the way usually followed, and common

characters which are not homologous are sometimes attributed to "mere convergence." It appears that there is more joy amongst morphologists over one attempt at genealogy than over ninety and nine demonstrations of convergence. Personally, I take the view that both of the above-named divisions of morphology are equally important.

There are several ways of convergence and' each is expressed in various degrees of intensity. The two most widely diffused ways of convergence are known respectively as homoplasy and mimicry.

True mimicry is defined by Mr Alfred Russel Wallace as "a form of protective resemblance in which one species so closely resembles another in external form and colouring as to Karl Semper, "The Natural Conditions of Existence as they affect Animal Life." Fourth edition, London, 1890.

The term and idea of homoplasy were introduced by Sir E. Ray Lankester: "On the Use of the Term Homology in Modern Zoology," *Ann. Nat. Hist.,* 1870. A. R. Wallace, " Darwinism." Second edition, London, 1890. be mistaken for it, although the two may not be really allied and often belong to distinct families or orders." The first constant condition under which true mimicry occurs is "that the imitative species occur in the same area and occupy the very same station as the imitated." The last essential condition of mimicry, as explained by Mr Wallace, is "that the imitation, however minute, is external and visible only, never extending to internal characters or to such as do not affect the external appearance." Furthermore, it is explained that warning coloration is the basis of the phenomenon of mimicry, but it is not stated what lies at the root of warning coloration. Of course it is fostered by natural selection, but we do not know the fundamental reaction that determines it. Professor Poulton adds as another attribute of true mimicry that it is a sham, that is to say, a false alarm; true warning colours, occurring in unpalatable or dangerous bodies, are genuine.

Warning coloration, mimicry, protective resemblance, and the death feint, are facts in nature which are known to have been doubted in the past by "armchair philosophers." This has doubtless been due to the fact that some delicate shade of meaning has often been overlooked in the original descriptions. Even if E. B. Poulton, "Colours of Animals," *Encyc Brit,* ninth edition, Supplement.

MOMENTS OF CONVERGENCE 55 both form and colour of a mimic harmonise with its model, there must still be some slight movement, some particular action or habit to complete the illusion. Thus, to take one example only as the type of a long series, there occurs in Ceylon a longicorn beetle, *Callichroma chrysogaster,* sufficiently rare to satisfy Wallace's condition that the imitators are always less numerous than the imitated, which shows characteristic waspish marks, orange yellow antennae and legs set upon a body uniformly bluish black above; but it only resembles a wasp when it is in flight and at the moment of alighting on a bush in full sunlight; when pinned in a box it is a "mere beetle."

Amongst insects especially there are many examples of forms belonging to different orders, protected by different noxious secretions, and yet possessing common warning colours, which do not occupy identical stations. Thus a Reduviid bug living under dry bark may resemble a Bombardier beetle living under damp logs. This belongs to Poulton's category of synaposematic resemblances "such as obtain between animals of all kinds adopting sematic signalling methods of defence in the same country"; this is sometimes known as Miillerian mimicry, as distinguished from true or Batesian mimicry. The common cryptic or protective coloration of many animals (oceanic, deserticolous, lichenicolous) in a special environment produces likenesses among different animals which are incidental and analogous to those convergent resemblances " caused by functional adaptation, such as the mole-like forms produced in the burrowing Insectivora, Rodentia, and Marsupialia" Poulton.

We may safely claim that the possession by noxious animals of common warning coloration is as much due to convergence as is the possession by harmless animals of_a._common protective coloration; and both of these colour-schemes are referable to conceivable though indefinite reactions. On the other hand, the resemblances and associations between palatable and unpalatable insects are hard to explain on the tropism theory, unless we suppose that they arose by ordinary convergence before advantage was taken of them by natural selection. We may therefore differentiate usefully between passive or convergent mimicry (including Poulton's syncryptic and synaposematic categories) and active or selective mimicry (including true mimetic resemblances); and we may add that while in typical cases the categories are sharply divided, in less obvious cases it is often as difficult to separate pure convergence from either form of" mimicry as it is to distinguish it from homology; the temptation being to describe the more or less sensational instances and to ignore those which are less convincing, thereby imparting a PHYSIOGNOMY 57 one-sided and exaggerated impression to a very common natural phenomenon.

Mimicry, in the wide sense of the term, involves the entire superficial aspect of the body; the moment the details are analysed the likeness disappears; it is absolutely essential to its success that structural details should be disregarded. We may define mimicry broadly as a physiognomical "convergence "TieFweerL IwoL.or more species of animals, in this way distinguishing it from homoplaiy, which depends upon a more deep-seated organic or structural convergence. Such coincidences of form and function as those presented by the mole-like burrowing mammals referred to above, by other marsupial and placental mammals, and by some arboreal mammals, *e.g.,* Tupaiidae (treeshrews) and Sciurida e (squirrels), the flying Insectivore *Galeopithecus* and the flying squirrel *Pteromys,* in so far as the whole bodily appearance is involved, afford examples of a third way,

of cony_ergence known as parallel evolution; it will I soon be clear how convergence is not incompatible with.parallelism. They resemble each other because of their approximation to fundamental forms, *e.g.,* the burrowing form, the arboreal form, and so on. A carnivorous Marsupial must necessarily bear some resemblance to a true Carnivore, the fact being that it is an extraordinarily close one.

There are very many examples, chiefly amongst insects and other arthropods, at all stages of growth and metamorphosis, of resemblances to fragments of vegetation, excrescences on bark, droppings, etc. It is usually not difficult to discriminate between effective resemblances which are objective, and fanciful resemblances which are subjective. With the latter I have nothing to do here, although they are sometimes of such a nature as to have given rise to enduring popular traditions, and on that account are entitled to respect within their own scope.

The resemblnnrp to n eommTm-fundamenlal form is well illustrated by the leaf-miniigs, of which the best known are the Leaf Butterflies and the Leaf Insects. Mr Wallace remarks that "many butterflies, in all parts of the world, resemble dead leaves on their under side, but those in which this form of protection is carried to the greatest perfection are the species of the Eastern genus *Kallima."* This genus of butterflies is noted for the extreme amount of individual variation in the markings on the under side of the wings, simulating all degrees of decay and discoloration and fungusattack; to this must be added the perfect leaf-shape and veining of the closed wings. Besides all this, its method of alighting is such as to complete the illusion. Referring in particular to the Sumatran species Wallace says that "this is effected by the butterLEAF BUTTERFLIES 59 fly always settling on a twig, with the short tail of the hind-wings just touching it and forming the leaf-stalk." In Sumatra he has often seen one enter a bush and then disappear like magic. In this account one may wonder why the butterfly resembles a dead leaf seeing that it rests upon a twig in the attitude of a normal leaf; perhaps it may be explained by the circumstance that in tropical vegetation a regular leaf-fall is the exception instead of being the rule as it is in temperate climates, and it is a very common thing to see a few conspicuously discoloured leaves still attached to the branches in the midst of green foliage.

The *Kallima philarchus* of Ceylon seems to behave rather differently since, as Mr E. E. Green has noticed and recorded, it "more usually settles head downwards on the trunk of a tree,... swaying gently from side to side. It might then be mistaken very easily for a detached leaf that in its fall has hitched up in a cobweb and is being shaken by the breeze." Another observer, Mr W. A. Cave, reports that he had exceptional opportunities for watching one of these butterflies at close quarters, as it frequented a certain spot on the trunk of a tree for two days; as soon as it settled, "which it did in the usual way, it immediately turned round so that its head pointed downwards." Mr Cave was much E. E. Green, "Mimicry in Insect Life, as exemplified by Ceylon Insects," *Spolia Zeylanica,* vol. v., 1908, *see* p. 89. W. A. Cave, Note on *Kallima philarchus, t. c.,* p. 142.
puzzled over this proceeding, which occurred every time the butterfly settled, until he discovered the reason: "the butterfly turned round so that the tail of its two hind wings would almost come into contact with the trunk of the tree, thus representing a stalk, and the apparently dead leaf would hang in a perfectly natural way, drooping downwards."

A Mexican leaf butterfly *Tagetis mermeria),* according to Mr C. W. Beebe, behaves in such a manner as to cause itself to be mistaken at first glance, not only for a fallen but for a falling leaf as well. Here also the individual variation is very great, in correspondence with the "variety of hues and mottlings which exist among dead and withered leaves.... When the insect took to wing it shot almost straight upward, and instantly attained the highest point of its flight. From here to its place of alight-

ing its course was a gradual descent—this living leaf unconsciously reflecting every detail of the fall of the withered bits of vegetation. And further, when the butterfly alighted, it was not with a fluttering and a few moments of hovering, but as a leaf comes to rest, so the insect—a sudden drop to the very ground, wings snapped together, and the apparently dried, worm-eaten leaf leaned far over to one side and swayed with every breath of air."

It is interesting to remark that a notion exists to the effect that the constant repetition of such C. William Beebe, "Two Bird-Lovers in Mexico," Boston and New York, 1905; *see* pp. 241-243. considerable variations as are met with in leaflike Lepidoptera and Orthoptera, from generation to generation, is a standing witness against the truth of "Darwinism," inasmuch as, according to the Darwinian theory, such variations ought either to become fixed by natural selection or swamped by interbreeding. On the face of it there would seem to be some force in this argument. Whatever the answer may be, it is not that these varieties may become fixed in course of time; on the other hand, it may be that natural selection is interested in keeping alive the variations for the benefit of the species, not for the production of new species. In any case it is a good point, worthy of special consideration.
Butterflies owe their leaf-like appearance to the effect of bilateral compression when the wings are closed. Leaf insects of the genus *Phyllium,* which belong to the order Orthoptera (containing also the cockroaches, grasshoppers, and stick-insects), owe it to the dorsiventral flattening of the body. A similar antagonistic flattening of the body occurs between two human ectoparasites where the compression also achieves a cryptic object indirectly, viz.: the bilaterally flattened *Pulex* and the dorsiventrally flattened *Cimex.*

An excellent description and plate of *Phyllium crurifolium,* a wonderful leaf insect which is found in the Seychelles islands as well as in Ceylon, has been published recently by Mr H. S. Leigh, whose account, based on material ob-

tained from the Seychelles and bred in England, I can confirm, having reared them in Ceylon for several years. The body of the males is generally green with a pair of clear ocellations on the fourth abdominal segment; they vary very little in colour; they have small tegmina and large wings, and are capable of flight; their legs break off by autotomy with the greatest ease. The flightless females, on the contrary, appear in two principal varieties, green and red (ferruginous), the green individuals predominating over the russet, but I have been unable to determine any constant numerical relation between them. The russet forms are more variegated and show more individual variation than the green forms. Out of one hundred and eight individuals reared from eggs laid by green females, six russet forms appeared after the later moults; out of seventy-five individuals reared from eggs laid by two russet females, one russet form appeared.

The female leaf insects therefore resemble both green and sere leaves in about the same proportion as the latter occur on green trees in the tropics. Not only this, but when immature they can fold up their abdomen like a curled leaf; and at all stages they sometimes sway like leaves in a breeze, and at other times remain H. S. Leigh, "Preliminary Account of the Life-History of the Leaf Insect, *Phyllium crurifolium* Serville," *P. Zool. Soc.,* London, 1909, pp. 103-113.

rigid with fore-limbs extended like leaves in a calm. The adult females, as duly noted by Leigh, are more sluggish than the males; and perhaps connected with this circumstance is their much lower capacity for autotomy of the appendages. A female can be held by the legs without discarding them, but if a male be so held mutilation ensues. The eggs of *Phyllium,* as of all Phasmidae, resemble plant seeds.
I may mention here an observation bearing upon the autotomy of the wings of termites. When they alight upon the ground after swarming out of the nest, it is well known that they throw off their wings by a special act of autotomy; but

if seized by the wings before the performance of this act, they cannot accomplish it so long as the wings are held. It is the same when only one wing is taken between the fingers; the autotomy is inhibited. The casting of the wings by termites and by ants is of course not followed by a corresponding act of regeneration, such as follows upon the autotomy of the legs of immature phasmids; mature male phasmids, as we have seen in the case of the leaf insect, cast their legs but will not live long enough to regenerate them.

Amongst fishes the Australian "Seahorse" The newly-hatched young of *Phyllium crurifolium* present a warning scheme of coloration which disappears with the first moult, blackish head and legs and a scarlet abdomen. I brought a quantity of eggs recently from Ceylon to England, some of which hatched out during the voyage, others later in the Zoological Gardens. On showing them fresh out of the egg to my friend Mr R. I. Pocock, he remarked instantly upon their striking resemblance to certain plant bugs.

Phyllopteryx, of which there is a figure in Dr Giinther's "Study of Fishes" (1880), is furnished with cutaneous processes which resemble trailing seaweed. Another fish, during a limited period of its life-history, namely, about the yearling stage, effectively resembles a dead water-logged leaf. This is the young of the so-called seabat, *Platax vespertilio* The mature fish is nearly uniformly dark-coloured; it attains a moderate size and is very high in the body, which is strongly compressed. It swims about in. small shoals and has the habit, possessed by many other similarly constituted fishes, of turning over on one side momentarily whilst swimming. In the young stage, when the total height of body and fins is about two or three inches, the colour is pale yellowish or brownish with variegated, irregular and variable markings. When seen living in the water, its resemblance to a sere leaf is extraordinary; when taken out of water it loses something of the strangeness of its appearance, and when preserved, the fins collapse, thereby de-

stroying the living aspect of the animal. In February 1904 I had the opportunity of seeing the peculiar movements of a young *Platax* under normal conditions, off the west coast of Ceylon. Whilst a fisherman was attempting to catch it with a pole-net, it suddenly toppled over A. Willey, " Note on Leaf-Mimicry," *Spolia Zeylanica,* vol. ii., 1904, pp. 51-55. *See* also *Nature,* vol. lxxx., 1909, p. 247.

LEAF FISHES 65 and sank gently and inertly to the bottom like a yellow leaf, for which I mistook it at first. As I was about to turn away from such a commonplace object as a drenched leaf, it righted itself once more and darted away. It was subsequently captured and sketched.

Fallen leaves of various kinds are commonly seen drifting about in the sea, sometimes at a considerable distance offshore. The most familiar examples of such drifting leaves are those of the mangrove trees which fringe the borders of estuaries and backwaters in the tropics. This singular Leaf Fish, besides having the requisite shape and colour, has also the power of assuming the inertia of a dead leaf, or of feigning death in the sea, thus completing the disguise. The contour of its body is strengthened behind by a line of dark pigment, which passes along the hinder margins of the dorsal and anal fins, but through the base of the caudal fin; the latter is unpigmented, hyaline and invisible under water. The pectoral fins are also transparent, but the elongated ventral fins are opaque, showing the yellow ground colour and a dense outer border conterminous with the border of the anal fin. There can be no mistake as to the effectiveness of this case of leaf-mimicry under water; moreover, the surface of the body shows lines of pigment and small spots such as are seen in a decaying leaf (Fig. 1).

The three different types *Phyllium, Kallima,*

E and *Platax,* which have so little in common otherwise, agree in exhibiting the shape of a

Fig. I. The Leaf Fish or yearling stage of *Platax*

vespertilio. Original from Spolia Zeylanica.

simple bifacial leaf, one of the commonest objects, dead or alive, ashore or afloat, in nature.

Yet they do not effectively resemble each other except in an abstract manner by conforming to a fundamental pattern, *i.e.,* by convergence.

The death feint is a common and very widely

COINCIDENCE AND CORRELATION 67 spread method of protection from predatory enemies. It is an extreme manifestation of the virtue of immobility which is equally well known to hunters and to their quarry. ffihen it js asjgid&ted-wjth singularities of form and coloration, it produces a combination wrnch' is so remarkable that IF is gerieralty a proper amount of scepticism. The resemblance whiciu-these,. animals bear to a leaf is a. selective one; that which they bear incidentally to each other is a convergent one, due to their independent acquirement of a common fundamental form. In these cases it may be supposed that natural selection has taken advantage of a previously existing aptitude, the essence of the leaf-form being present as a generic character before the actual assumption of the intimate resemblance became fixed.

Other striking convergences depending upon form and coloration are those which obtain between some harmless and some poisonous snakes inhabiting the tropical regions of both hemispheres. Darwin described the examples from South America. The mutual resemblances proceed largely from the character of the transverse banding of the body which they have in common; and the colour coincidence may be so close that in a rapid sorting the species would be thrown together and confounded one with another.

Lastly, reference should be made to the wellknown cases of plumage resemblances amongst birds and to the longitudinal striping of some mammals, *e.g.* , young wild pig, young tapir, mouse-deer, striped squirrels, etc. In all these cases convergence is independent of selection.

In order to guard against conveying a wrong impression, it may be well to add that in cases of double or multiple convergence such as are mentioned on p. 52, there is no *a prion* presumption of correlation between the several characters which are repeated in the different types. Thus there is no correlation between the separately moving eyes of *Hippocampus* and its prehensile tail, because other Lophobranchiate fishes (Pipe-fishes), which have a straight tail, roll their eyes in the same way, as can be seen very prettily in the Naples Aquarium. The property which these fishes present in common with chameleons is the possession of exceptionally sluggish habits; and the extreme mobility of the eyes compensates for the relative inflexibility of the body. Nor is there any correlation between the oviposition of the Platypus *Ornithorhynchus)* and the shape of its bill; the latter is correlated with its aquatic and feeding habits. The conjunction of characters may be a coincidence; the repetition of the coincidence is an act of convergence. For a discussion of correlation between teeth and limbs in the evolution of Mammalia *see* Professor H. F. Osborn's paper on "The Law of Adaptive Radiation," *American Naturalist,* vol. xxxvi., 1902, pp. 353-363.

CHAPTER VI DIVERGENCE AND PARALLELISM

Few things are more astonishing at first acquaintance than examples of close convergence, whether mimetic or homoplastic, because they appear paradoxical and contrary to expectation. In fact the ways of convergence are devious, many-hued, illuminating, full of surprises, inviting away from the narrow path of homology which, at least in extreme cases, begins and ends in obscurity. It must, however, be acknowledged that the pioneer work which effected the discovery of the pelagic larvae of so many marine animals about the middle of the nineteenth century, was thoroughly satisfactory, and seemed to indicate to a later generation that the pursuit of homology as an aid to phylogeny was not wholly elusive. If there has been any mistake it has been

that of not defining the different degrees of homology. But there is no necessity to dwell upon mistakes nor to regret them.

As a seeming paradox there comes the pre liminary axiom that convergence-depends firstly on divergence and secondly on parallelism. As 69 E *2* we ascend higher in the scale of nature we find that the co-ordinating mechanism of the animal body keeps pace with the rest of the organisation, and the leading members of the several *phyla* or branches of the animal kingdom become ever farther removed from each other and from what

Fig. 2. Diagram of phyletic divergence and parallelism.

we may designate vaguely as their common starting-point. Thus the highest Mollusca, the Cephalopoda (squids, octopods, cuttle-fishes, and Nautilus), which are characterised by a high degree of cephalisation or concentration and PARALLEL DIVISIONS 71 amalgamation of parts to form the head, represent the maximum organic development within the Molluscan phylum, and are therefore farther removed from the highest mammals than is the lowly *Chiton,* because the Mollusca and the Vertebrata have been advancing along indgr penHpnt parallel lines. and the cephalisation with its implied brainpower, is an act of convergence.

The Molluscan and Vertebrate phyla, and all the phyla, although their actual origins are lost in Silurian darkness, may or must be supposed to have diverged from a common base in the first instance. This point is illustrated graphically in Fig. 2; and the same principle of primary divergence and secondary parallelism will apply to each phylum (Figs. 3 and 4). Nothing in phylogeny seems more firmly established than the pelmatozoic ancestry of the Echinoderms (star-fishes, sea-urchins, etc.), nor than the bilaterally symmetrical ancestry of the Pelmatozoa, the former deduction largely resulting from their paleontology, the latter confirmed by their embryology.

As for the Vertebrata, not all of them possess vertebrae, but all have a noto-

chord. The term

Protochordata, with the subsidiary terms Urochordata (for the Tunicata or Ascidians) and Cephalochordata (for the Acrania or Amphioxus), was introduced by Balfour in his "Comparative Embryology" in 1882. Subsequently in 1884 Bateson suggested the additional term Hemichordata for the Enteropneusta (" Balano *Cf.E.W.* MacBride, "Echinodermata" in *Cambridge Natural History,* vol. i., 1906.

MECHANISM OF NUTRITION 73 glossus "). Dr Gaskell has reversed the position by the recent statement that a large number of zoologists, who consider the notochord as a great characteristic of the vertebrate organisation, have followed Bateson in the matter of terminology.

Taken as a whole the habits of animals are cast into certain well-defined moulds, and it is quite easy to understand why this should be so; but the much more apparent than real simplicity of the matter is no reason why it should not be stated at length. Animals differ from plants in their nutrition, mobility, and sensibility. The manner in which the nutrition of animals differs from that of green plants is sharp and unequivocal, so much so that it can be expressed in two contrasting terms, holozoic and holophytic, between which extremes, however, all grades of what is known as mixotrophism (mixed dietary) are to be found, chiefly but not entirely amongst the lower orders.

Green plants alone can elaborate their own food, with the help of the sun, from inorganic substances; animals require their food ready made before they can begin to assimilate it. Plants have only to assimilate, and that in one way; animals have first to procure their food, and that in many ways. And yet there is as W. H. Gaskell, "Origin of Vertebrates," London, 1908, *set* p. 16.

much relative diversity amongst plants as amongst animals, showing that differentiation proceeds from within though it may be modified from without. The methods adopted for securing food determine in great measure the habits of animals. Their instincts and intelligence are concentrated upon their food-supply, reproduction being automatic and all besides incidental. It is small wonder then that many animals follow similar methods; and in this way habitual convergence is brought about. Thus the carnivorous, insectivorous, herbivorous, and frugivorous habits are widely disseminated; and community of habit and experience is often accompanied by greater or less similarity of structure of certain parts, giving rise to a twofold exhibition of convergence, bionomical and homoplastic.

Next to the function of nutrition we have to consider the organs which perform that function, *i.e.,* the mechanism of nutrition. For the sake of brevity we may concentrate our attention upon the higher or leaf-bearing plants and the higher or gut-bearing animals. Now some parasitic plants, the so-called rootparasites *(Balanophora, Rafflesia),* can manage without green leaves, and some parasitic animals, both endoparasites (Cestoda and Acanthocephala) and ectoparasites *(Sacculina),* can dispense with a gut. When, however, as in the great majority of vascular HOMOLOGY OF THE GUT 75 plants, true foliage leaves occur, they are homologous throughout. Sometimes other structures (cladodes and phyllodes) can function as leaves, *i.e.,* as organs of assimilation; but the special homologies of certain leaf-like structures do not affect the general homology of leaves, which is one of the cardinal points in vegetable morphology. The distinction between the special homology of parts and the _general homolog-yufjhe whole rjegjaires toi_be_emphasised.

The special morphology of the alimentary tract of animals is a large subject which demands exhaustive analysis; but it is distinct from the question of the general homology of the gut. It is probable that no single division of an insect's gut, for example, can be strictly homologised with a corresponding part of a fish's gut, but looked at in their entirety, the general homology of the one with the other is still a question apart, to be answered by an appeal to first principles. That it must be answered one way or the other is evident from the fact that

objections have been raised against the alleged view 'Lthat the one organ which is homologous throughout 'the animal kingdom is the gut," Gaskell, *l.c..* This is perhaps an extreme way of putting it, but we may examine the point very briefly, always bearing in mind the distinction between special and general homology.

Dr Gaskell regards the nervous system as constituting the master tissue of the animal body, and there is no doubt that he is right up to a certain point. The behaviour of Protozoa and Sponges in this regard, however, teaches us that in the course of evolution the nervous mechanism is secondary as compared with the mechanism of locomotion on the one hand, and nutrition on the other. An obvious rejoinder to this argumentation might be that the organisation of Protozoa and Sponges also teaches us that the gut, as an organ, is secondary to nutrition as a function. That this is so is borne out by the fact, referred to above, that just as in plants certain structures which are not leaves have secondarily acquired the function of leaves, so amongst animals the parasitic Cestode and Acanthocephalous worms, which have secondarily lost the use and presence of a gut as a consequence of their mode of life, absorb fluid nutriment, prepared by the host, through the outer surface of the body. Here therefore the body-wall does duty for the gutwall, combining the somatic and splanchnic functions into one.

We are therefore driven to enquire whether the general homology of the gut of triploblastic (three-germ-layered) animals still retains its dominance, like that of the foliage leaf, in spite of exceptional cases and special homologies. The only reply to this imaginary question that CONVERGENT METAMERISM 77 presents itself to my mind is this: — The integrity of the gut throughout the Triploblastica cannot be assailed without invalidating the continuity of the archenteric cavity or primitive gut throughout the Metazoa; but this is to strike at the root of the entire fabric of comparative morphology, since the archenteron is as much the palladium

of animal morphology as the primitive leaf-member is the rootconception of botany.

The Triploblastica are composed of two great series representing distinct phyletic types, namely, the Platyhelminthes and the Coelomata. The highest flatworms, the Nemertina, show points of convergence towards Coelomata just as the highest Mollusca, the Cephalopoda, show points of convergence towards Vertebrata.

Inseparable from the question of the general homology of the gut in coelomate animals is that of the general homology of the coelom or secondary body-cavity itself. It must suffice here to affirm this general homology, again on first principles; but just as the divisions of the gut are obviously not homologous throughout the coelomate series, neither are the subdivisions of the coelom, *i.e.,* the somites, necessarily homologous. A phenomenon analogous to metameric segmentation is that of strobilation, which is definitely known to occur independently in different phyla, *e.g.,* Coelenterata, Platyhelminthes, Annelida. In some Annelid worms, *e. g.,* Syllidse, strobilation is superadded to the normal segmentation. As I have indicated in the diagram (Fig. 2), the Appendiculata are here regarded as a parallel stem to the Vertebrata, having a common Coelenterate origin. This scheme is in accordance with the conviction that the somites of Annelids and Arthropods have been evolved along their own line of descent, independently of the somites of Vertebrata.

The metamerism of Appendiculata and Vertebrata is therefore, on this view, a conspicuous example of convergence, and as such I regard it, taking into account the facts which have been made known concerning it. If this view is correct, as I believe it to be, there can be no question of comparing the regional differentiation of Arthropods, such as Limulus and the Scorpion, with that of Vertebrata. The whole comparison, except by way of a possible convergence here and there, is ruled out of court. The existence of convergent strobilation is in itself presumptive evidence of the possibility of convergent metamerism, and there are other facts which render it extremely probable and, to my mind, practically certain.

Instances of parallel convergence are so numerous and so common that we begin to realise that convergence is a regular and not an exceptional phenomenon. The most striking MAMMALIAN CONVERGENCE 79 example of the three principles of divergence, convergence and parallelism, at one and the same time, is of jLQursejLhaL-which-is-afforded by the parallel series presented by the Marsupial Mammals or Metatheria, on the one hand, and

—-s».

the ordinary Placental _ MammalsMor _Eutheria-en, the other. I have compiled a table and give a graphic representation of it in Fig. 5. The inward bends of the parallel waved lines indicate particular features of convergence selected for the purpose of the diagram. A similar diagram could be constructed for comparing the series of Insectivora and Rodentia, the spiny armature of the hedgehogs approximating to that of the porcupines, the arboreal habit of tree-shrews (Tupaiidae) to that of squirrels (Sciuridae), the terrestrial, nocturnal, and semi-domesticated habit of land-shrews to that of mice and rats, while the aquatic habit and the parachute flight are also met with in both orders. The musk-shrew, *Crocidura murina,* is very rat-like in general deportment, although its eyes are small and its dentition that of Insectivora.

Parallel evolution accompanied by convergence is the expression of analogous formations in two or more animals belonging to different subdivisions, which may have acquired a similar differentiation of outward appearance or internal The items are gathered from Flower and Lydekker's textbook on Mammals, with reference also to Max Weber's " Saiigethiere." organisation independently along different lines of descent, the points in which they resemble each other giving no indication of genetic affinity nor even of bionomical association.

The general resemblances cited above relate

Fig. 5. Parallelism with convergence amongst mammals. M = Marsupials; P = Placentals. This phenomenon was observed by Cuvier and by Owen. The habits which lie at the base of the convergence in each case are indicated by the numbers:— 1. Carnivorous. 2. Ant-eating (myrmecophagous). 3. Flying. 4. Swimming. 5. Burrowing (large-eyed forms). 6. Burrowing (small-eyed forms). APPENDICULATES AND VERTEBRATES 81 to the external configuration of the body, and some of them at least are sufficiently remarkable, not to say astonishing. Perhaps one of the closest degrees of functional convergence is that which is manifested between the appendiculate (annelid and arthropod) and vertebrate central nervous systems, upon which attention has been focussed by Dr Gaskell. The central nervous apparatus is the dominant system in the organisation of the higher animals, and he thinks that it has been a dominant factor in evolution. The comparison tabulated below from Dr Gaskell's recently published volume on the "Origin of Vertebrates"(London, 1908) appears to me to serve as a most beautiful example of true physiological convergence, but likely to be confounded with the spurious convergence presented by the so-called cephalic stomach of the arthropod in comparison with the ventricles of the brain in the craniate vertebrates. Now, it may appear something like an impertinence to describe as a spurious convergence what Dr Gaskell regards as a true homology; it is, however, nothing of the kind, and is no more than an expression of the opposite point of view. On that understanding we may leave it for the present, perhaps returning to it later, either directly or by implication. TABLE OF CONVERGENCE IN THE STRUCTURE OF THE CENTRAL NERVOUS SYSTEM (NEURAL CONVERGENCE)

Appendiculate. *Segmented invertebrate).*

I. Supra-oesophageal ganglia, giving origin to the nerves of the eyes and antennules, *i.e.,* the optic and olfactory nerves.

i. Circum-cesophageal commissures

connecting the cerebral ganglia with the infra-oesophageal ganglia and the ventral chain. 3. Infra-cesophageal ganglia and the paired ventral chain of segmental ganglia. Each pair of ganglia gives rise to the nerves of its own segment, motor and sensory; by the agency of which food is ingested, respiration and locomotion effected. Vertebrate. *Craniate vertebrate).*

1. The brain proper from which arise only the olfactory and optic nerves. 2. *Crura cerebri,* strands of fibres on each side of the infundibulum, connecting the higher brain region proper with the lower region of the medulla oblongata and spinal cord. 3. Region of the midbrain, medulla oblongata, and spinal cord; from these arises a series of nerves segmentally arranged, which, as in the invertebrate, give origin to the nerves governing mastication, respiration, and locomotion.

With reference to the first sub-heading in the above table it is to be remarked that Dr Gaskell duly points out that the crustacean antennules are olfactory in function, but he does not add that they are also the carriers of the auditory organs and that the latter are innervated from the cerebral ganglia as they are in Mollusca. At the same time a physiologist may be pardoned for regarding the close correspondence as a manifestation of homology rather than as a case of APPENDICULATES AND VERTEBRATES 83 convergence.; and there are other facts which serve still more to complicate the issue and to baffle the most competent judgment. Chief amongst these is the apparent topographical coincidence between the infundibulum in the floor of the third ventricle of the vertebrate brain and the appendiculate oesophagus.

If we admit the convergence as tabulated above, why should we not regard this further coincidence as another case of convergence? There are at least two reasons why I think we should not: firstly, because the structural convergence in the two types of central nervous system is accompanied by a certain degree of functional equivalence, whereas the topographical coincidence of infundibulum and oesophagus is not accompanied by any functional equivalence; secondly, because the infundibulum can be brought into interesting topographical correlation with a primitive feature quite different from the appendiculate oesophagus, namely, the anterior neuropore or anterior neurenteric canal of protochordates. If the striking correspondence in plan of composition of the central nervous system in appendiculates and vertebrates had been recognised as an instance of general structural convergence thirty-five years ago, when the late Dr Anton Dohrn, the founder of the Stazione Zoologica at Naples, explained his application of the principle of change of function in relation to the origin of vertebrates (1875), it would not have led to what many zoologists are constrained to regard as a series of false homologies; and *per contra* it would not have led to many interesting discoveries.

There are two factors which conspire to beguile a morphologist into spurious relations and vain imaginings: these are the potency of convergence and the weight of coincidence. A very eminent French zoologist, who enjoyed the respect and veneration of all who came directly or indirectly within the sphere of his influence, the late Professor Henri de Lacaze-Duthiers, thought from the beginning to the end that the Ascidians (Tunicata) are related to the Mollusca. In apparent confirmation of this belief he discovered the case of a simple Ascidian, a species of *Molgula,* which develops without the intervention of the usual tailed larva; and then he discovered a form in the Mediterranean which he called *Chevreulius,* but which had already been named *Rhodosoma* from the Pacific, where the atrial and buccal siphons lie within a hinged valve which can be opened and closed like the valves of a lamellibranchiate mollusc.

It is indeed extraordinary to relate, in Dr Gaskell's words, that the infundibulum "lies just anteriorly to the exits of the third cranial or oculomotor nerves; in other words, it marks the termination of the series of spinal and cranial VERTEBRATE DESCENT 85 segmental nerves.

... Not only, then, are the nerve-masses in the two systems appendiculate and vertebrate exactly comparable, but in the very place where the oesophageal tube is found in the invertebrate, the infundibular tube exists in the vertebrate. ..." All this is true, but what Dr Gaskell does not relate at this crucial point of his narrative *(l.c.,* p. 14) is that the infundibulum also occurs essentially at the same horizon, with reference to the segmental nerves, as the anterior neuropore and olfactory pit of Amphioxus, where there are likewise two anterior pairs of sensory cranial nerves terminating in peripheral ganglion cells on the praoral lobe.

It is not particularly edifying to pursue one phantom rather than another; and the spirit of morphology may be said to reside not so much in a desire for ultimate truth, that is to say, to attain the unattainable, as in the will to accept nothing but the truth. Applying this aphorism to the special case of the two opposing theories of vertebrate descent, namely, the Appendiculate theory and the Protochordate theory, we may say that if the latter fails to satisfy, so at least does the former. It is necessary to codify the facts; but this can be done for the present upon a broad basis of convergence better than by an unrestrained use of homology.

Dr Gaskell's references to the anterior neuropore of Amphioxus occur on pp. 220 and 457 of his work, to which I refer the reader.

Meanwhile we may agree unreservedly with Dr Gaskell's opinion that nothing but good can result from the incursion of the physiologist into the realm of the morphologist. Then, and then only, do we begin to realise how we stand in regard to the facts of comparative anatomy, and to perceive the paramount importance of convergence.

With regard to the special case of the nervous system we must add that there is no ground for imagining that it is the one organic system throughout the animal kingdom which offers no instances of convergence.

CHAPTER VII SPECIAL CONVERGENCE

Special convergence depends npnn.

iuwtmnal 7alence,_which may or may not h§ arrnmjjanied by partial homology. The different degrees may be expressed in various ways at convenience, according as it is desired to focus attention upon a function or an organ, or upon the systematic position. In the systematic method of arrangement one makes use of the terms employed in classification. Individual or racial convergence refers to those resemblances between varieties of a species such as are familiar in the human race as the so-called "doubles." Specific, generic, family, ordinal, class, and phyletic convergence refer respectively to the species of a polytypic genus, to the Since the above was written Professor Adam Sedgwick has kindly drawn my attention to a paper by Professor Arthur Keith on "The Position of the Negro and Pygmy amongst Human Races" in *Nature,* vol. lxxxiv., 1910, p.54. Professor Keith thinks that pygmies, who are widely distributed, are "modifications produced locally from the larger negro.... The Congo pygmies share all the physical features of the Bantu except size; the Bushman has the characters of the Hottentot, while the pygmies of the Far East find their nearest representatives in the negroes of Oceania. " genera of a family, to the families of an order, to the orders of a class, to the classes of a phylum and to the phyla of the animal kingdom.

One of the best examples of special family convergence is afforded by the pectoral fins of flying fishes. Semper *(pp. cit.)* dealt with the organs of flight in Vertebrata, and figured a flying "herring," *Exoccetus,* belonging to the Teleostean family Scombresocidae, in juxtaposition with a bat; but he did not refer to the case of the flying gurnard, *Dactylopterus,* which belongs to another family, the Triglida e (sometimes called Cottidae and Cataphracti). Both of these genera occur in the Mediterranean as well as in the Indian Ocean, and are totally different from each other, not only in systematic position but in external form. *Dactylopterus* has a broad, depressed head, armed with powerful spines, on account of which the head is commonly fractured by a blow when the fish is caught by native fishermen off the coast of Ceylon; the scales are hard, keeled scutes; the tail-fin is truncated, the abdomen flattened, and the body coloured red. *Exoccetus* has a normal herring-like head and body, unarmed, with smooth scales, a deeplyforked tail-fin, a convex abdomen, and a silvery ground colour. Both kinds of flying-fishes owe their limited power of flight above the surface of the sea to the secondary elongation and WING FLIGHT 89 expansion of the pectoral fins, an exceptional modification which has been acquired independently within the limits *of iy/b* very distinct families.

It is remarkable to find such strictly homologous organs as the pectoral fins of Teleostean fishes modified in a virtually identical manner to perform a special and exceptional function, whose transformation is nevertheless not homogenetic but homoplastic. This typical example serves to illustrate one of the most interesting manifestations of convergence, namely, the homoplastic modification of homogenetic structures.

The comparison between the wings of birds and of bats offers different conditions. They are equally efficient as organs of sustained aerial flight; they. show. complete functional equivalence j the fore-limbs are homologous; but the transformation has proceeded along divergent. lines, an expanded Wing-membrane or patagium with reduced epidermal appendages (hairs) in the one case; a rudimentary patagium and enlarged epidermal appendages (feathers) in the other; with corresponding differences affecting the skeleton of the wing-supporting limbs, hypertrophied digits in the bat, atrophied digits in the bird. Unlike the flying fishes, the modification has not taken place in an identical manner, but in an almost diametrically opposite manner; it cannot therefore be described as homoplastic in the strict sense of the term, although it is frequently quoted as a stereotyped example of homoplasy. Perhaps it would be more logical to express it in other language for which a suitable technical term does not seem to be available, unless we may borrow a word from another division of the subject and call it a heterotypic modification of homogenetic structures, the common starting-point being the-pentadactyle limb ot terrestrial vertebrates.

Birds and bats are directly comparable in terms of the theory of convergence, not only because they are alone amongst vertebrate animals in their capacity for rapid and changing flight, but also because they are both warm-blooded. Flying fishes bear the same relation to birds as they do to bats, whatever that relation may be held to be. In my opinion they are in no way comparable, inasmuch as the flight of fishes is of the nature of a parachute flight and so belongs to a different category. Although well enough twenty years ago, it would not be admissible to-day to figure a flying fish and a bat upon the same page for the purpose of illustrating the principle of homoplastic wing-formation, except in respect of the one point of the hypertrophy of the pectoral rays and digits. It would be more appropriate to present a flying fish in conjunction with a flying lizard, or even a flying squirrel, the nature of the relation between them being one of general functional convergence, neither associated with PARACHUTE FLIGHT 91 homology nor with general structural convergence or homoplasy.

The case of *Pteromys* and *Galeopithecus,* quoted above, may be regarded as an example of the homoplastic modification of homogenetic structures in different orders,_z.g.ordinal_convergence; but the homoplasy, in the literal sense, is not complete, since there are important differencesofstjucturaJejl thedlglts of *GrtfeopiiJiecus* being webbed, and the wrist of *Pteromys* carrying an accessory cartilaginous rod which gives material support to the parachute.

The degrees of convergence are endless and can 6hTy"be classTEeaTni a broad way; it is, we may repeat, a fundamental phenomenon and.CQHrsequently of frequent occurrence, though not always equally demonstrative. Very striking are those cases where special features which are exceptional within a certain limited systematic range are repeated independently, as the phosphorescent and electric organs of fishes. The late Professor Howes, in one of his addresses, quoted as a critical example of convergence the fact that the Mesozoic reptiles yielded terrestrial, aquatic, and aerial forms, just as did the Tertiary mammals which replaced the former in order of dominance.

Amongst animals which are more or less Flower and Lydekker, "Mammals Living and Extinct," London, 1891, Fig. on p. 615.

nocturnal in their habits, he pupil of the eye becomes contracted in a. bright light to a narrow aperture which may retain its normal and primitive circular shape or may become a vertical ellipse or a narrow vertical slit or a horizontal ellipse or slit. The pupil of the cat's eye is round at night time, vertically contracted during the day; the leopard's eye and the jaguar's, on the contrary, like the lion and tiger, contract in bright sunlight to a circular pinhole aperture. Mr Frank Buckland has noted that the pupil of the fox's eye behaves, not like the dog's, as one would expect, but like the cat's, and this linear pupil is, by some writers, advanced as a generic character of the genus *Vulpes,* as distinguished from *Cants.*

Amongst tailless Batrachia (frogs and toads) the most extensive genera, *Rana, Bufo, Rhacophorus* and *Ixalus,* have a horizontal pupil, a vertical pupil being the exception in this division. Geckoes (Geckonidae), the lizards of tropical and subtropical countries which can run along upright and over-hanging surfaces by virtue of the adhesive pads on their digits, have the vertical form of pupil; when partially contracted the margin of the iris in some species is crenulated; and when quite contracted so that the anterior and posterior borders are in contact, leaving only a vertical pupillary suture between them, the *E.g. *, E. T. Seton, " Life-Histories of Northern Animals." New York, 1909, 2 vols. latter has a beaded appearance, the beading corresponding with the previously noted crenulations. Crocodiles also show the narrow vertical pupil.

Among snakes, round and vertical pupils occur with nearly equal frequency, the former rather more frequently than the latter; but *Dryophis,* called the whip-snake, has a very pronounced horizontal pupil (Fig. 6).

In the class Mammalia the round pupil prevails, whereas the vertical pupil, as mentioned above, characterises certain groups. The oblong horizontal pupil of the horse, camel, ox, and sheep was referred to by Owen in his "Anatomy of Vertebrates" (1866); it is very sharply defined in goats that have a gilt-edged iris. Owen also stated that in a dead Agouti (Rodentia) the pupil was a horizontal ellipse; but he did not allude to the horizontal pupil of the mungoose, nor have I seen it mentioned in any other work so far as I can remember. In the Civet family (Viverridae), which is closely allied to the Felidae, the vertical pupil appears to be the rule, but *Herpestes,* the Indian mungoose, has a welldefined, horizontal pupil in the daytime, becoming round at night (Fig. 7, *Frontispiece).* The allied genus *Suricata,* the South African meerkat, has a similarly shaped pupil, shown very clearly in the specimens at the London Zoological Gardens. Hubrecht *I.c.,* 1908) has given reasjQns_Jbr believing that the cartilaginous fishes orr"py a side branch of the vertebrate stem, and he goes so far as to ""gg"'_.? rgdiral rnangp in the classification of vertebrates-, dividing them into four superclasses: Cephaloch ordata *Amphi*ar«. y),Cyclostomata (lampreys, etc.), Chondrophora (sharks, etc.), and Osteophora (bony fishes and higher vertebrates). In view of this weighty opinion, the *a priori* probability that the nictitating membrane of some sharks (Carchariidae), which is an accessory protection for the eye, sweeping over the surface of the eyeball, has no genetic connection with the functionally equivalent membrane of many of the higher vertebrates, is greatly strengthened.

Bony fishes have no movable eyelid _s»__hui transparent adipose eyelids are sometimes present, composed of an anterior and posterior membrane or of a continuous circular membrane perforated at or about the centre. Both the Grey Mullet family (Mugilidae) and the Herring family (Clupeida) are respectively differentiated into groups by the presence or absence of adipose eyelids which must have arisen independently in those families. Where there is a continuous perforated membrane, as in some Clupeidae *(e.g., Dussumieria,* Fig. 8), the condition presented calls to mind that of the Oegopsid cuttlefishes, where the outer covering of the eye is likewise perforated. No doubt the two conditions are physiologically comparable.

Fig. 8. Eye of *Dussumieria* showing perforated adipose eyelid. The outline of the pupil is seen below the transparent dotted adipose membrane.

Raptorial or prehensile appendages amongst invertebrate animals offer further analogies. Chelate extremities occur alike in Crustacea and Arachnida; and the characteristic clasp knife appendages of the Stomatopod Crustacea *(Squilla)* are found again in Orthopterous insects (Mantodea) and in Neuropterous insects (Mantispidae). In *Chiromantis,* a tropical African genus of frogs allied to *Rhacophorus,* the two inner fingers of the hand are opposite and opposable to the two outer fingers, so that its structure resembles that of the grasping hand of chameleons. All these cases belong to the great category of opposable extremities, some of which are G. A. Boulenger, *Catal. Batr. Sal,* 1882, p. 92, pi. x., Figs. 1 and 2. reciprocally homologous, whilst others, like the above, are homoplastic.

Another case worth quoting, as well known to students of osteology as it is remarkable, is that of convergent opisthocoely already mentioned by Owen' as occurring in the North American freshwater Ganoid fish, *Lepidosteus* the Garpike, in the Surinam toad, *Pipa americana,* and in the Salamanders. In Batrachia and Reptilia the vertebrae articulate together by a cup-and-ball or ball-and-socket arrangement, and, as a general rule, the cup lies at the front end of the centrum of each vertebra to receive the condyle which projects from the hinder end of the preceding vertebra. Such vertebrae with the concavities in front are called procoelous. In rare cases the reversed condition obtains, where the condyles project at the front ends of the vertebrae and fit into the cups at the hinder ends of the preceding vertebra. Such vertebrae with the concavities behind are called opisthocoelous.

The vertebrae of fishes are joined together by ligament, and the centra do not possess articular surfaces; both in front and behind there is a deep cup, whence the vertebrae are designated amphicoelous or biconcave. *Lepidosteus* is unique amongst existing fishes in having opisthocoelous vertebrae. The same description of vertebrae only occurs otherwise in certain Batrachia, in R. Owen, "Anatomy of Vertebrates," London, 1866,1, pp. 33-34.

OPISTHOCOELOUS VERTEBRA 97 eluding the newts and salamanders among the Urodela, and a number of genera of Anura of peculiar habits belonging to separate families and each containing a single species, namely, *Bombinator* the European Fire-bellied toad, *Pipa* the Surinam toad, *Alytes* the Midwife toad, and *Discoglossus,* the Painted frog, a circum-Mediterranean batrachian. The opisthocoely of *Pipa* is probably independent of that of the other named Anura; that of the named Anura collectively is probably independent of salamandrine opisthocoely; and Batrachian opisthocoely as a whole is independent of that of *Lepidosteus.*

Somewhat analogous to the reversed articulation of vertebra? described in the preceding paragraph is the reversed spire of the shell in Molluscs and the reversed pose of the body in Flatfishes. These two latter cases of *situs inversus* were quoted by Bateson as examples of discontinuity in substantive variation, but they must be mentioned again here as examples of convergent variation. "In both of the groups named, some species are normally right-handed, others being normally left-handed, while as individual variations reversed examples are found.... The fact that the reversed condition may become a character of an established race is familiar in the case of *Fusus antiquus*. This shell is found in abundance as a fossil of the Norwich Crag, such specimens being normally

G left-handed, though the same species at the present day is a right-handed one." In India and Ceylon, where the chank shell *(Turbinella pyrum)* plays such a large part in religious ceremonies, the rare apparition of a sinistral form is regarded as a favourable portent, and such a shell is very highly esteemed. There would appear to be some common causes operating during the early development to procure such cases of reversal. A spiral shell can only be twisted in one of two directions; and a Pleuronectid fish can only lie on one of two sides. These alternative conditions, one of which is frequently the rule, the other the exception, afford an interesting sidelight upon the incidence of convergence.

The classification of reversed molluscs' is the same in principle as that for reversed flatfishes, namely:— (1) Cases in which the genus is normally sinistral. (2) Cases in which the genus is normally dextral but certain species are normally sinistral. (3) Cases in which the species is indifferently dextral or sinistral. (4) Cases in which a sinistral form is an abnormal monstrosity. W. Bateson, "Materials for the Study of Variation," London, 1894, p. 54. *Cf.* A. H. Cooke "Molluscs," *Cambridge Natural History*, 1895, p. 249. TEN-LEGGED PANTOPODS 99

A striking example of generic convergence is exhibited in the ten-legged Pantopods or "seaspiders" which have been obtained from the South Polar region by the English and Scottish National Antarctic Expeditions. They belong to two quite distinct genera, *Pentanymphon* Hodgson, 1904, and *Decolopoda* Eights, 1837; the former only differing from *Nymphon* by its possession of an extra pair of legs; the latter most nearly related to *Colossendeis*, from which it differs likewise by its possession of an extra pair of legs, and also by the presence of a pair of well-developed, three-jointed mandibles. These two Antarctic genera are thus nearly

related to two other representative Pantopod genera but not to each other. Professor D'Arcy Thompson places them in widely separated families: Decolopodida? and Nymphonida; and Schimkewitsch has arrived at the same conclusion, namely, that the ten-legged Pantopods do not constitute a distinct group in contrast with the more usual eight-legged forms, but that they arose independently from eight-legged forms, the number of legs giving no clue to their affinities.

The following table, compiled from the data furnished by Hodgson, who collected and D'Arcy W. Thompson, "Pycnogonida," *Camb. Nat. Hist.,* iv., 1909, pp. 531 and 537.

W. Schimkewitsch, " Uber die Periodicitat in dem System der Pantopoden," *Zool. Anz.,* xxx., 1906, p. 3. Besides the Reports of the Voyages, see the following papers described *Pentanymphon* during the National Antarctic Expedition in the *Discovery,* and redescribed *Decolopoda* from material procured by Mr W. S. Bruce during the Scottish National Antarctic Expedition in the *Scotia,* shows the radical differences which exist between the two genera simultaneously with the numerical convergence of the ambulatory appendages. The differential characters indicate the respective places of the genera in the system of Pantopoda; the convergent character gives no indication of their affinities to any existing forms. TABLE OF CONVERGENCE IN PANTOPODA.

	Pentanymphon.	Decolopoda.
1.	Ambulatory appendages, five pairs.	Ambulatory appendages, five pairs.
2.	Body elongate, clearly segmented, very slender, with lateral processes widely separated.	Body short, obscurely segmented, broadly elliptical including the lateral processes in the contour of the ellipse.
3.	Proboscis cylindrical, straight, much shorter than the body.	Proboscis clavate, bent downwards, longer than the body.
4.	Mandibles chelate, 2-jointed.	Mandibles chelate, 3-jointed.
5.	Palps S-jointed.	Palps 10-jointed.
6.	Ovigerous legs, 10-jointed, formed plainly as in *Nymphon.*	Ovigerous legs, 10-jointed, looped as in *Colossendeis.*
7.	Abdomen small, ovoid, subdirected obliquely upwards.	Abdomen long, slender, clavate.

by T. V. Hodgson: 1. "On a New Pycnogonid from the South Polar Regions," *Ann. Nat. Hist.* (7), xiv., 1904, pp. 458-462, pi. xiv. 2. "Scotia Collections. On Decalopoda australis Eights, an old Pycnogonid rediscovered," *Proc. Roy. Phys. Soc.,* Edinburgh, vol. xvi., 1905, pp. 35-42, pi. iii. 3. "Decalopoda and Colossendeis," *Zool. Anz.,* xxix., 1905, pp. 254-256. The accepted spelling of the former name is now *Decolopoda.* TEN-LEGGED PANTOPODS 101

This table shows two genera belonging to different families of a comparatively small order, with one very prominent character in common which cannot be referred back to a common origin.

Quite recently a letter from Dr W. T. Caiman, containing further references to Antarctic Pantopoda, appeared in *Nature* (vol. lxxxiv., 28th July 1910, p. 104), which adds to the importance of this case. A third genus of ten-legged Pantopods, named *Pentapycnon* by Professor E. L. Bouvier, has been obtained by Dr Charcot's expedition in the *Pourquoi Pas,* and "strange to say, it appears to be quite unrelated to the other two. *Pentapycnon charcoti* is a near relative of *Pycnogonum,* hitherto regarded as the most highly-specialised of all Pycnogonida. Further, just as *Pentanymphon* is accompanied by a species of *Nymphon,* and *Decolopoda* by *Colossendeis,* so Professor Bouvier finds that *Pycnogonum,* hitherto unknown from Antarctic seas, is represented by a new species alongside of *Pentapycnon* at the South Shetlands."

We may now consider the case of two genera of toads belonging to one family (Bufonidae) of a large order (Batrachia-Anura). These show several exceptional characters in common, side by side with a number of strongly divergent features. The divergences in structure and distribution are so great as to make it doubtful whether any of the other characters are traceable to direct genetic affinity; and Gadow suggests that their community of habits with concomitant modifications of structure may be due to convergent evolution. The structural features in the table given below are taken from Boulenger; the feeding habits are gathered from Gadow. Both of these authors note their resemblance to the firmisternal family of Engystomatidae, on the one hand, and their systematic position under the arciferous Bufonidae, on the other. The vertical pupil of the eye is an exceptional character among the Bufonidae.

TABLE OF CONVERGENCE IN BUFONIDAE.

Myobatrachus. Rhinophrynus. 1. Distribution. Australia. Mexico. 2. Shoulder girdle. Epicor-The same, except sternum acoid cartilages narrow and rudimentary. scarcely overlapping; no omosternum; sternum (or metasternum) cartilaginous, ossified or calcified on the median line. 3. Eye. Pupil vertical. Pupil vertical. 4. Ear. Tympanum distinct. Tympanum absent. 5. Tongue small, elliptical, Tongue elongate, subtrianentire and free behind. gular, free in front. 6. Fingers and toes free. Fingers free, toes webbed. 7. Limbs very short, adapted Limbs very short. for burrowing. 8. Male with a subgular vocal Male with two lateral vocal sac. sacs internal behind the angle of the mouth. 9. Habits. Feeding on ter-Feeding on termites and ants, mites and ants. H. Gadow, "Amphibia and Reptiles," *Camb. Nat. Hist,* 1901, pp. 166 and 227. G. A. Boulenger, *Catalogue Batr. Sal.,* 1882, pp. 328-329. PLACENTATION 103

The phenomena of placentation, according to Hubrecht, are "intimately related to the higher development which characterises the mammalia as against the lower Vertebrates." This means that the intensive nutrition of the embryo is a prior condition to the development of brain power, and it should be kept in mind as a counterpoise to Gaskell's opinion that the brain power is the primary directive influence in evolution. We may indeed state the case outright by saying that cerebral concentration is the end and not the beginning of evolution.

The history of the mammalian placenta affords many examples of convergence. Diffuse placentation, in which the surface of the maternal uterine mucous membrane is thrown into a dense network of folds and crypts into which corresponding folds or villi, diffused over the entire surface of the blastocyst, fit without any strong adhesion to the uterine wall, has usually been regarded as a primitive condition; and the arrangement seen in the horse and the pig has always been looked upon as the prototype of the diffuse placenta. Hubrecht, however, gives weighty reasons for thinking that it is due to a secondarily simplified process, or descent with simplification, in the course of which the intense phagocytic activity of the trophoblast or outer fœtal envelope had subsided and had given place to a diffused osmotic activity usually accompanied by great increase in the size of the blastocyst.

Similar simplification and change of function leading to parallel results have occurred in other orders of mammals, *e. g.,* in certain Edentates *(Manis* the pangolin, or scaly ant-eater) and in the Lemurs. Hubrecht expresses the hope that his discussion of the facts will prevent any future attempt to place Ungulates and Lemurs on the same level of so-called primitive placentation.

In the same way the old hypothesis which maintained that the early villiferous state of the human blastocyst, in the phase called " Reichert's ovum," recapitulates ontogenetically a diffuse phase to which the discoid stage succeeded later, ought to be discarded, because, *inter alia,* Reichert's ovum is enclosed by a *decidua refiexa seu capsularis,* and is not freely suspended in the uterine cavity as are the blastocysts which show diffuse placentation. Furthermore, Hubrecht adds that this "phenomenon of encapsulisation inside the mucosa has appeared independently in more than one order of mammals." The arrangement in question, by which the developing blastocyst is withdrawn from the uterine lumen and enclosed by a *decidua capsularis,* has been realised in man and anthropoid apes, in different genera of rodents, in the spiny hedgehog *Erinaceus,* in the spineless Malayan hedgePLACENTATION 105 hog *Gymnu-* *ra,* and rather less completely in the Chiroptera (bats).

Similarly the discoidal form of the placenta gives no indication of affinity between the widely different mammals which present it. It is, as Hubrecht says, a temporary production, the discoidal shape being of no value when considering questions of affinity. He instances the discoid placenta of the mole out of which the allantoic villi are withdrawn at birth like the fingers out of a glove, the young when born being "enveloped in the allantois with the fully extracted villi forming a woolly covering to that foetal involucrum"; the discoid placenta of *Galeopithecus,* containing lacunae filled with maternal blood and imbedded in the uterine wall; "the discoid placenta of the rabbit and of *Tarsius* which, when full grown, is attached to the mother by a stalk of much smaller diameter than the placenta itself; the discoid placenta of the hedgehog and of man, the latter with its loose and floating villi as against the dense trellis-work of villi and trophoblast in the former."

Before leaving the subject of the nutrition of the young of vertebrates, one more matter may receive attention, namely, the secretion of milk that takes place in the mammary glands from which the mammalia take their name. According A. A. W. Hubrecht, "Early Ontogenetic Phenomena in Mammals," *Quart. Journ. Micr. Sc,* vol. liii., 1908, see pp. 70, 113, 129, 142, etc.

to Owen *(pp. cit.,* vol. ii. p. 160), John Hunter "made many interesting observations on the crop of pigeons, which takes on a secreting function during the breeding season, for the purpose of supplying the young pigeons in the callow state with a diet suitable to their tender condition. An abundant secretion of a milky fluid of an ash-grey colour, which coagulates with acids and forms curd, is poured out into the crop and mixed with the macerating grains. This phenomenon is the nearest approach in the class of birds to the characteristic mammary function of a higher class; and the analogy of the 'pigeon's milk' to the lacteal secretion of the mammalia has not escaped popular notice.... The secretion consists of proteine with oil, but contains no sugar of milk nor fluid caseine. "

An analogous secretion has been discovered by Alcock to take place in the uterus of viviparous rays. In pregnant females of sting-rays *(Trygon)*, of the eagle-ray *(Myliobatis)*, and in the bat-ray *(Pteroplatcea)*, Alcock found that the young are nourished before birth by a milky secretion that exudes from glandular filaments or villi on the inner surface of the uterine wall, a large bundle of the filaments passing through each spiracle into the pharynx of the immature fish. The milk-secreting filaments are penetrated by a capillary network in the meshes of which the milk-glands are imbedded. Each filament SECRETION OF MILK 107 is provided with superficial muscles whose contraction must serve to squeeze the milk out. These vascular villi give a shaggy appearance to the mucous membrane of the oviduct, and Alcock describes them as "dripping with milk" and discharging a creamy, albuminous fluid. This method of intra-uterine nutrition of the young by a special secretion of the uterine glands offers at once a great contrast and a remarkable parallel to the corresponding phenomena in mammals.

Every system of organs throughout the animal kingdom will be found to yield abundant instances of convergence. An excellent example of what may be called gastral convergence is exhibited in the structure of the gizzard of some Teleostean fishes. In the first place, as between the pyloric gizzard of the few fishes which possess one and the pyloric gizzard which is so characteristic of birds, it is to be noted that the most absolute comparability prevails, differences in detail notwithstanding. They are homoplastic modifications of a homologous structure, namely, the pyloric division of the vertebrate stomach. The exceptional occurrence of a gizzard in fishes and the regular presence of one in birds give no more indications of affinity than does the gizzard of A. Alcock, "A Naturalist in Indian Seas," London, 1902, *see* pp. 71, 159, 210. This valuable book contains a bibliography of the published work of the Indian Marine Survey ship *Investigator.* Compare also the gizzard of the toothless Ant-eaters.

the earthworm or that of some molluscs. The latter are examples of phyletic convergence not based directly on special homology; the gizzard in fishes and birds is a case of class convergence based, as we have seen, upon a homogenetic foundation. We may thus once more distinguish clearly between convergence with homology and that without it. This may seem rather paradoxical, but it is true and sufficiendy significant to bear repetition: the pyloric division of the stomach is homologous in fishes and birds; but the gizzard of fishes, which is a direct modification of the pylorus, is not homologous with the gizzard of birds, which is likewise a direct, though independent, modification of the pylorus.

In that rich storehouse of facts, Owen's "Anatomy of Vertebrates" (1866), the gizzard of the Grey Mullet *Mugil)* is thus described (vol. i. p. 418): "The cardiac portion here forms a long *cul-de-sac*; the pyloric part is continued from the cardiac end of this at right angles and is of a conical figure externally; but the cavity within is reduced almost to a linear fissure by the great development of the muscular parietes, which are an inch thick at the base of the cone; and this part is lined by a thick horny epithelium." In other cases the pylorus will be found to be hard and muscular, as in the Red Mullet (*Upeneotdes*). In the Clupeoid genus *Megalops,* the pylorus is a long, straight, porrect ascending tube, GIZZARD IN FISHES 109 rather hard at its distal extremity; in another Clupeoid genus *Dussumieria,* the pylorus appears as an arched muscular tube lying across the body cavity from left to right, the concavity of the arch being directed forwards (Fig. 9). In a species of Grey Mullet from Ceylon which I identified as *Mugil olivaceus* Day, I found the gastric ccecum rudimentary and the cardiac division of the stomach was followed by a round, white, muscular, bulbous gizzard; the intestine was full of fine sand; six pyloric cceca embraced the gizzard; another specimen had only five pyloric cceca. What, however, surprised me very much at the time—and I have not found it mentioned in any work which I have consulted since—was the discovery of an almost precisely similar gizzard intestinal tract of in a Clupeoid fish, *Cnatoessus* pirus. *nasus,* which frequents the same g-c-Gastric cardiac , 1, ccecum.

back-waters as the grey mullet. *p,* pyloric cceca. In this species *C. nasus)* the . stomach is frankly destitute of a cardiac ccecum, and terminates in a round, muscular, red, bulbous gizzard. In one of the specimens dissected, the gizzard and intestine were full of fine sand as in the mullet; and the presence of sand was noted in the pyloric cceca. The latter arise in tufts along the length of the duodenum (Fig. 10).

Fig. Io. Dissection of the alimentary tract of *Chaioessus nasus* from the left side. The dotted line indicates the cut edge of the body-wall.

1. Gall-bladder. 2. Visceral nerve lying upon the cardiac tube of the stomach. 3. Air-bladder. 4. Ductus pneumaticus. 5. Pyloric gizzard with a tuft of coeca projecting in front of it. 6. Duodenum (green-tinted when fresh). 7. Rectum. 8. Hind-portion of left testis. 9. Vas deferens.

Here, then, we have two fishes belonging to widely separated families, though pursuing similar habits, and presenting independently an identical modification of the pyloric division of the stomach. I confess that at first acquaintance with this case I began to distrust my own eyes; perhaps it will not strike the reader of these pages so forcibly; but I submit it as one of the most stringent object lessons in homoplasy imaginable.

It may be admitted that wherever there is a GIZZARD IN FISHES in distinct pyloric division of the stomach, the material for a hard muscular gizzard exists. It is obvious that the constitution of the alimentary canal depends upon the nature of the food. Comparative anatomy and physiology teach us that the digestive tract reacts to different conditions of nutrition; but not many such unequivocal demonstrations of the independent acquisition, within the limits of an order, of a compact specialised structure as that described above, can be pointed to.

Regarding the families of the Mugilidae and Clupeidae in their entirety, we have now considered two characters with respect to which they converge, namely, the adipose eyelids (above, p. 94) and the pyloric gizzard. In both of these cases, as well as in that of the pectoral fins of the flying fishes, we have anatomically identical structures arising independently from a common origin. Facts of this nature apparently take the ground away from any intelligible conception of homology—but only apparently. The relations can be illustrated graphically, as shown in the diagram (Fig. 11).

The gizzard of the mullet was known to John Hunter, who tells us that of all the fish seen John Hunter, "Observations on the Gillaroo Trout, commonly called in Ireland the Gizzard Trout," *Phil. Trans.*, 1774; reprinted in his "Animal Oeconomy," which was republished in vol. iv. of Hunter's Works, edited by James F. Palmer, 1835-1837. Here also is to be found Hunter's paper, "On a Secretion in the Crop of Breeding Pigeons, for the Nourishment of their Young." by him the mullet offered the most complete instance of this structure, its strong muscular stomach being evidently adapted, like the gizzard of birds, to the two offices of mastication and digestion. The stomach of the gillaroo trout, in

Fig. Ii. Parallelism with convergence between two families of fishes, Mugilidae and Clupeidae.

Hunter's experience, held the second place. But the gizzard of *Chatoessus*, described above, holds a position of equality with that of the mullet.

It should be added that Darwin ("Origin of Species," p. 235) referred to the luminous organs of insects of distinct families and diverse topography as a phenomenon parallel with that of the electric organs of fishes.

CHAPTER VIII

Habitudes And Attitudes
(bionomical Convergence)

Identity of habitat occasions convergence of habits on the part of diverse animals. A great deal of this has been implied in the preceding chapters, but more remains to be said. The three principal functions of animal life, at least above the level of the sponge, are metabolism, reproduction, and neuration, the last being at once the master and the servant of the others, and leading on from a lower to a more advanced cerebration. The number of phyla or leading types of the animal kingdom is considerable, and there are only these three primary functions upon which to ring the changes.

If there is one aspect of convergence more widespread than another, it is that of cerebral convergence, which is associated with the phenomenon of cephalisation or head-formation; and we can infer from this circumstance how hopeless must be the search for neural homology as Metabolism comprises nutrition, respiration, and excretion. between parallel types of the animal kingdom. The cerebration of the ant is comparable, in several of its manifestations, with that of the higher mammals, but its evolution is distinct and its mechanism different. The comparison between the two forms is most profitable in the abstract; but it points away from homology, not towards it. Perhaps either direction leads round in a vicious circle to the same goal, namely, the point from which we started; but we may gather much by the way if we do not stray too far from the track and lose ourselves in a jungle of facts and speculations.

National life is chiefly controlled by the desire to capture markets. Animal life is chiefly concerned with the occupation of feeding grounds. In general, any given feeding area can support a very mixed population, and the association of forms which batten upon any particular source of supply constitutes what has been termed the bioccenosis Dahl of that centre. This community of interests is a phase of symbiosis or commensalism, not based upon mutual advantage nor even upon mutual tolera-

tion, in the first instance, but upon strict independence and selfhelp.

All the species which take part in such associations may be said to converge towards a common centre of sustenance, and it is generally, though by no means invariably noted that the assemblage ECTOPARASITES 115 is a heterogeneous one, the species composing it belonging to so many genera, and the genera usually belonging to different families or orders. How far this community of habitat leads to structural convergence is not clear, because the anatomical characters of the associated forms have not been worked out in sufficient detail from this point of view. A case in point is the overlapping of head and pronotum in some ectoparasitic insects to which attention has been drawn recently by Dr K. Jordan. In *Arixenia*, an apterous earwig found in the nursing pouch of the naked bat of the Sunda Islands, the occipital margin of the head is slightly concave, without a sharp edge, and is not closely applied to the pronotum. In *Hemimerus*, another apterous earwig bearing a superficial resemblance to some Blattidae, from the African murine genus *Cricetomys*, the hind edge of the head projects backwards, overlapping the pronotum to a slight extent. Dr Jordan adds that this overlapping, which is exceptional among insects, is best known in fleas and in some Hemiptera parasitic on bats. In the beaver parasite, *Platypsyllus castoris*, the head and pronotum fit well together, and there is a comb of spines extending from the edge of the head on to the thorax, bridging over the gap which might be formed when the head K. Jordan, "New Apterous Earwig *Arixenia),' Novitat. Zoolog.*, xvi., 1909, p. 318.

is bent down. The overlapping between head and pronotum of parasites which live in the fur of mammals renders the surface uniform and more suitable for gliding through the fur, and is a secondary development which has taken place independently in these not nearly related insects Jordan, *loc. cit.*.

The identification of the species of arthropods, land-planarians, earthworms, and molluscs found in or about a single fallen log is a matter of almost unspeakable difficulty under the present conditions of zoological nomenclature and publication. By far the greatest amount of biological interest connected with a particular species may be due to the association under which it was found, but this is a matter of the least possible systematic importance, except in the case of parasites. The mere commingling of different forms, apart from structural details, constitutes a phase of our subject which is worthy of notice, and may be termed bioccenotic convergence.

It is known and will be found recorded in Darwin's "Monograph of the Cirripedia," that barnacles are frequently found attached by their peduncles to the skin of sea-snakes (Hydrophidae). Occasionally a considerable cluster of barnacles may be fixed upon the flattened tail of a slender snake, as in the case of a *Hydrus platurus* Such expressions as this are introduced merely for convenience of reference and classification of the phenomena, ASSOCIATIONS 117 from the coast of Ceylon, now preserved in the Colombo Museum, whose tail was beset with a group of barnacles composed of two species, *Lepas anserifera* and *Conchoderma kunteri.* The barnacles are not ectoparasitic, since they do not feed upon the skin of the snake nor do they assist the snake in any way; on the contrary, their presence must have seriously impeded its movements. This snake is sufficiently protected from larger enemies by its warning coloration (black and yellow) and by its possession of poison fangs. Moreover, the barnacles thrive equally well when attached to floating bottles and drifting spars, and the sea-snake in question was merely their facultative vehicle.

The relation of barnacles to the skin of seasnakes is somewhat analogous to a remarkable case of association between certain Hydroid polyps *(Stylactis minoi)* and a small rock perch, *Minous inermis,* which has been found in several places off the west coast of India at depths of 45-150 fathoms. The skin of the fish is beset with the commensal polyps which have never been found elsewhere, and Colonel Alcock *pp. cit. , 1902)* thinks that they help to conceal the fish from its enemies, in that they play the same part which is, in other cases, performed by frond-like, cutaneous filaments. In both cases feeding is carried on independently of the vertebrate host. The barnacles, named above, are sedentary animals that require to be kept in motion at the surface of the sea; while the hydroid is a sedentary species which requires an adventitious mobility at the bottom of the sea.

The Tubificidee are a family of small freshwater Annelid worms, allied to earthworms, which live in the mud of water-courses, sometimes occurring in almost pure cultures of innumerable individuals. They keep the head and forebody buried in the mud, whilst the hinder portion of the body, through which respiration is effected, is kept constantly waving as near the surface of the shallow water as possible. When alarmed, an entire colony will instantly withdraw out of sight into the mud as with one consent. Living in the same environment and sometimes in company with the worms are to be found the larvae of midge flies *(Chironomus).* They have the same habit of waving the body in the water and the respiratory processes occur at the hinder end; and, most singular coincidence of all, the blood of the insect larvae is coloured red with haemoglobin like that of the worms.

In his description of the larva of *Chironomus,* commonly called the "Bloodworm," Professor Miall (" Natural History of Aquatic Insects," London, 1895) says: "When undisturbed, they The habit of waving the posterior end of the body in the water has been noted for *Tubifex rivulorum* by L. Atheston, *Anat. Anz.,* xvi., p. 497; I have observed it in the case of an unnamed species of *Limnodrilus* from Ceylon, as described in the text SOCIAL INSECTS may often be seen to push the head-end well out of the burrow for purposes of feeding; at other times the tail-end is pushed out and waved to and fro in the water, as a help to respiration." This may be compared with Atheston on *Tubifex:* "It forms flexible tubes open at both ends, of particles of soil cemented by mucus. When contracted, the worm lies wholly within the tube. When active, the posterior end (third or half of the body) projects into the water, waving about in a rapid, undulatory manner, while from the other end of the tube is protruded the anterior end of the worm which is thrust about through the mud in search of food." *Limnodrilus,* as observed by me in Ceylon, forms dense aggregates of individuals surrounded by mud, but does not form definite tubes which can be isolated from the clumps.

No example of bionomical convergence is more remarkable than that which is presented by the social insects, ants, bees, wasps, and termites. The termites so much resemble ants in their mode of life and social organisation that they are commonly known in the tropics as white ants, though they are not ants and are not always white. Not only have they no direct genetic relationship with the true ants (Formicidce, order Hymenoptera), but the latter are among their most formidable enemies.

A minute ant will overpower a termite twice or three times its own size, seizing it from behind round the middle, causing it to twist and writhe, but never loosening its hold upon the doomed victim. The social differentiation of workers, soldiers, kings, and queens is the same in the ant family and in the termite family; but the feeding-habits are quite different, and termites do not keep slaves. The nearer relationships of the termites are with cockroaches and earwigs. Froggatt thinks that the discovery of the giant termite from Port Darwin, *Mastotermes darwiniensis,* "brings them almost into touch with the family Blattidae."

Although termites do not employ slaves as some ants do, yet they entertain guests which are known as termitophilous insects, as distinguished from the myrmecophilous insects which frequent ants' nests. Interesting exhibitions of mimicry and other special adaptations result from these associations. The phase of mimicry which involves the assumption of the ant-facies is called myrmecoidism by Wasmann. He distinguishes passive mimicry, or the deceptive resemblance of the outward form, from active mimicry, which consists in an imitation of the behaviour of the hosts. The mimicry which has Walter W. Froggatt, "White Ants." Department of Agriculture, New South Wales. Miscellaneous Publication No. 874, 1905; containing a bibliography of papers dealing with Australian termites. MYRMECOIDISM 121 r for its end the deception of the hosts is further distinguished from other forms of myrmecoidism amongst Arthropoda; one phase of the latter is merely a morphological family resemblance without apparent biological significance.

Some guests are welcome, others are hostile. An example of the latter is a small beetle, *Myrmedonia,* some species of which are myrmecophilous, whilst others are termitophilous. They lie in wait in obscure corners of the nest, whence they fall upon isolated ants and tear them to pieces; on the other hand, they have much ado on their part to escape the vigilance of the warrior ants. The myrmecophilous species of *Myrmedonia* resemble the ants with which they associate both in colour and in form; so much so that Wasmann himself has been repeatedly deceived at a first glance. The object of this mimicry is demonstrated by Wasmann to be the optical delusion of the ants.

Among the numerous Oriental species of termitophilous *Myrmedonia* there is no such mimicry, although the *Termes* soldiers are as capable of defence as are the ant soldiers, but with this difference, that they are completely blind. In the nests of the termite genus *Hodotermes,* whose soldiers possess well-developed, facetted eyes, no *Myrmedonia* has been found. E. Wasmann, "Die psychischen Fahigkeiten der Ameisen," second edition. Published in *Zoologica,* Bd. xi., Heft 26. Stuttgart,

Another phase of bionomical convergence is that contained in the phenomena of direct and indirect development amongst many invertebrate animals.

Direct development is straightforward, gradual, without striking metamorphosis, and must be regarded, in a certain sense, as normal. Works which deal with direct development are apt to become standard and classical; they give the clue to fundamental homologies and generalisations. The theory of the coelom could hardly have been established upon an indirect course *i* of development; and on the other hand, the relationship between the Enteropneusta and Echinodermata would not have been recognised so easily from the direct development, although the larva of *Asterina gibbosa* would doubtless have called for comparison with Bateson's larva of Balanoglossus. The differences between the larvae of certain marine organisms consist in the littoral or stereotropic habit of the direct forms as contrasted with the pelagic or free-swimming (pleotropic) habit of the indirect forms; and they are anticipated by the size of the egg and the amount of food yolk it contains. A very small egg will develop into a pelagic larva; a relatively large egg will develop directly into a larva in 1909, pp. 190, 5 plates. Contains bibliography of Wasmann's numerous contributions to the knowledge of myrmecophily and termitophily.

11 employ this name in the old sense, just as Amphioxus is still extensively used, without trenching upon questions of nomenclature. TORNARIA 123 which the form of the adult can be more or less clearly discerned, unless, as in the case of the above-named starfish, the adult form has suffered a peculiar change from a bilaterally symmetrical type.

The general name of the pelagic larval form of those Enteropneusta (Balanoglossida), which produce small ova not exceeding 0.15 mm. in diameter, is Tornaria. All members of the families Ptychoderidae and Glandicipitida (or Spengelidae) produce such eggs. The Harrimanidae produce large yolky eggs from 0.4 mm. in *Dolichoglossus kowalevskii* to as much as 1.5 mm. in *Stereobalanus kupfferi.* Tornaria was discovered in 1848 by the famous German physiologist Johannes

Miiller of Berlin, who thought that it was an Echinoderm larva; its real nature was determined in 1869 by Professor Elias Metschnikoff.

It is well known how much the quantity of food-yolk in the egg-cell affects the course not only of the segmentation-stages, but also of the subsequent embryonic and larval development; and that, under normal conditions of nutrition, the size of the *egg* is a fairly constant specific character.

The dimensions of the eggs of different animals do not always vary in proportion to the bulk of the progenitors. Amongst existing birds, where oviparity is the rule without any exceptions, the smallest species yield the smallest eggs and the largest birds lay the largest eggs, but the intervening sizes show great fluctuations, as may be seen by comparing the egg of a Megapode with that of a Jungle Fowl.

Amongst reptiles there are many exceptions to the rule of oviparity, but there is no known correlation between lecithality, or the relative quantity of yolk in the *egg,* and viviparity; this latter habit not leading to a reduction of the vitellus, although it may affect the shell-formation, causing the complete absence of calcareous deposits, so that the embryo shows clearly through its thin transparent envelopes. The intra-uterine development of a yolk-laden *egg* is a special phase of incubation or brood-nursing, and has been assumed independently by some arboreal and deserticolous lizards of diverse families in distant parts of the world.

A fundamental rule with regard to methods of propagation is that oviposition preceded viviparity, but this rule does not assist in determining whether the ancestors of a particular class were egg-layers or vivipars, and consequently whether the egg-laying members of a group where viviparity predominates are primitive in that respect. Lecithality, oviparity, and viviparity are or may be independent phenomena. It is probable, for QC A. Willey, 1906, "Viviparity of *Cophotis ceylanica* and Oviparity of *Ceratophora stoddartii" Spolia Zeylanica,* vol. iii., pp. 235-237 and figure.

PERIPATUS 125 example, that the egg-laying habit of the Australian monotremes is due to early regression or descent with simplification in a primitive type, while the lecithality of their eggs is not a palingenetic or high ancestral quality, but adaptive or cenogenetic. The abundance and scarcity of yolk may be alike primitive and secondary features within certain defined limits, in a manner analogous with the plurality and duality of teats in mammals.

It is not only among mammals that we find large eggs associated with oviparity and small eggs with viviparity and placentation; and not only among marine organisms do we find large eggs associated with direct development and small eggs with indirect development. *Peripatus* is a soft-bodied, cryptozoic animal, living in the tropics under logs and leaves, whose body has the consistency of a caterpillar, and whose feet are numerous like those of a centipede but not jointed. It is known by no other name except that of its own division of the Appendiculata, namely, the Onychophora. The class name Prototracheata was applied by Moseley to this group, but since that time it has been recognised that tracheate animals do not form a homogeneous series, as will be explained more fully below. This is Professor Hubrecht's view *(I.c., 1908). Cf.* A. Willey, "The Lacteal Tract of *Loris gracilis? Spolia Zeylanica,* vol. iii., 1905 (1906), pp. 160-162 and figure *4 fa,' _ 4".a*

The Onychophora furnish instructive gradations from placentation, at one extreme, to oviposition at the other, the sizes of the eggs increasing *pari passu* from minimal to maximal dimensions. The species show a peculiar correlation between their geographical distribution and their morphological differentiation; and to some extent, though not entirely, the modes of development vary with the distribution. The placental condition of the small-egged South American species is highly specialised; the oviparous habit of some Australasian species is, to my mind, clearly secondary. As for the species themselves, one form is not appreciably more primitive than another.

In this group, therefore, the two extreme methods of nutrition of the embryo are equally cenogenetic. There still remain three intermediate states of the embryo, namely, the trophoblastic development of the small-egged New Britain species, and also of a South African species; the normal or direct development of the Cape species; and the yolky or meroblastic development of some Australian and Malayan species.

Just as among aquatic organisms which discharge their spawn freely into the water, a *Cf.* Adam Sedgwick, "The Distribution and Classification of the Onychophora," *Quart. Journ. Micr. Sc.,* vol. lii., 1908, pp. 379-406. *Cf.* A. Dendy, "On the Oviparous Species of Onychophora," *Quart. Journ. Micr. Sc.,* vol. xlv., 1902, pp. 363-414. OPTIMUM CONDITIONS 137 distinction has to be made between direct and indirect development, so in the intra-uterine development of *Peripatus* a similar contrast occurs. What is meant by a normal course of development is one that is not disturbed by adventitious factors. We must assume certain optimum conditions which need by no means be the most primitive and indeed on *a priori* considerations are not likely to have been the earliest conditions encountered by the amphibious palaeozoic prototracheate ancestors of our terrestrial arthropods. Optimum conditions may be brought about by the acquisition of a little yolk in the egg or by the loss of a little yolk; and this may make a considerable difference in the behaviour of the embryos or larvae, as the case may be. All methods of development may be regarded as more or less cenogenetic, and the selection of a particular type as primitive may be purely arbitrary; but there can hardly be two opinions as to a normal or direct course which can be established as a legitimate standard or constant. Any life-history can recapitulate certain ancestral or palingenetic features, some more recent, others more remote. Different species may provide seemingly identical conditions for the maturation of the ova and the development of the young; but it does not follow that the reactions or adaptations to these conditions will be identical.

When both conditions and reactions in different specific groups are identical, convergence based on homology ensues. Thus the trophoblastic vesicle of *Peripatus novce-britannia* is doubtless homologous with that of the South African *P. sedgwickii;* but the adaptation which produced the structure out of the primitive matrix may have been evolved independently, *i.e.,* along closely parallel lines in the two species. If this is so it is an example of close specific convergence.

In accordance with the Trophoblast Theory, the trophoblast, wherever it occurs, is to be defined as an outer larval, or extra-embryonic envelope or appendage which has acquired phagocytic properties in order to provide for the intra-uterine nutrition of viviparous, terrestrial animals which have descended from oviparous, aquatic ancestors. In accordance with the theory of Larval Forms amongst aquatic organisms other than Arthropoda, what may be termed by contrast the kinetoblast or outer ciliated investment of the larva has acquired special locomotor properties, frequently concentrated along definite tracts, in order to provide for the pelagic life and independent nutrition of the young.

From whatever point of view the matter may be regarded, the parallelism between direct and indirect development in Enteropneusta and Onychophora, not to mention other cases, is a very suggestive one.

PALOLO 129

The swarming habit of some marine Annelids for the purpose of breeding is worth mentioning as affording a particularly interesting example of bionomical convergence. The celebrated palolo worm of Samoa and neighbouring parts of the South Pacific is the occasion, in Samoa, of an annual national festival owing to the regularity and abundance of its swarms and to its edible properties. It is eaten raw or baked in leaves of the bread-fruit tree, and the natives send presents of it to distant friends and to the chiefs. The most remarkable feature in the biology of the palolo *(Eunice viridis)* is its perfectly constant appearance in the months of October and November when the moon is in its last quarter.

S. J. Whitmee, who first reported upon this phenomenon in 1875 *Z00L Soc,* London, pp. 496-502), found that the palolo keeps astronomical time; as an indication of this it will suffice to quote the recorded fact that in 1874 it reappeared, after an interval of thirteen lunar months, on 31st October and 1st November. Nineteen years later, in 1893, Dr Kramer collected the material upon which A. Collin reported, again on 31st October and 1st November.

Subsequently an Atlantic palolo manifestation, occurring in the Tortugas during June and July, Ant. Collin, 1897, "Bemerkungen iiber den essbaren Palolowurm." In Kramer's " Bau der Korallenriffe." Kiel und Leipzig.

on the part of another species, *Eunice fucata,* was described by A. G. Mayer (1900); and later still a Japanese palolo, belonging to a different family (Nereidae), was described under the name *Ceratocephale osawai* by Izuka. The last-named author says that the swarming of the Japanese worm takes place in October and November during the nights closely following the new and the full moon, and it resembles that of the Atlantic and Pacific species in its general course, but differs in the circumstance that whereas in the species of *Eunice* the sexual segments occupy the posterior portion of the body which becomes detached from the headend at the time of swarming, in the Japanese worm the sexual segments are confined to the anterior portion which, at the swarming season, sheds the posterior, shrunken, asexual segments.

Amongst the numerous methods of broodnursing or care of eggs and young, we meet with some extraordinary cases of convergence of varying degree. Frequently they are obvious enough, but that very fact only serves to strengthen the argument which I am endeavouring to develop, that convergence is not a subordinate but a dominant factor in morphology. Firstly, let us take the phe-

nomenon of buccal Akira Izuka, "Observations on the Japanese Palolo," *Journ. Coll. Sct. Imp. Univ.,* Tokyo, 1903, vol. xvii., article II, pp. 1-37, 2 plates.

BUCCAL INCUBATION 131 incubation, well known in point of time, but not too familiar in personal experience. In Ceylon it was first described by the Rev. B. Boake (1867-1870) as occurring in the Siluroid fish *Arius falcarius,* which has been determined by Dr Francis Day to be synonymous with *Arius boakei.* This fish frequents estuarine waters and is very common in an extensive backwater on the west coast of Ceylon called the Panadure River. It has very large yolkladen eggs more than half an inch in diameter. After being laid by the female they are found nowhere except in the mouth of the male, where they remain until they are hatched and until the young have completely absorbed the yolksac. I have observed that the intestine of brood-nursing males is generally contracted to narrow dimensions and empty, a fact which was also noted by Day; and as generally, the palatine teeth of ovigerous males are greatly reduced. In one case, however, which came under my notice, where there were fifteen eggs in the mouth, each containing an advanced embryo, the palatine teeth were not appreciably reduced and the hind-gut contained *shell-dSrts.* The opening of the oesophagus is constricted and virtually closed, while the mouth and pharynx are expanded to form a spacious brood-pouch, where the eggs and young are exposed to a constant current of water which passes over them and through the gill-clefts of the foster-parent. Day observed the same incubation in the allied genus *Osteogeniosus,* and Dr Giinther and others had recorded them for South American species of *Arius?*

Over against the buccal incubation of fishes we may place that of the Chilian toad-like Batrachian, *Rhinoderma daiwini,* which was regarded as one of the most interesting finds of the voyage of the *Beagle,* although it is not mentioned in Darwin's "Naturalist's Voyage." The male of this toad possesses a median

gular sac, representing an extension of the buccal cavity, which opens by two apertures on the floor of the mouth. At the breeding season it becomes a large brood-pouch, lying freely in the ventral lymph-sinus and reaching back to the pubic region. Jiminez de la Espada, who first brought this fact to light in 1872, found as many as fifteen metamorphosing larvae in the broodpouch. Howes dissected a male in 1888 which contained eleven larvae; unlike the eggs and fry of *Arius,* these larvae were unequally advanced, only five of them being still provided with a tail.

Espada noted a shrinkage of the viscera as if the foster-parent had ceased to feed during the In the Japan-British Exhibition (1910) specimens of a Nile fish, *Tilapia nilotica,* are exhibted by Mr C. L. Boulenger, showing females carrying their eggs and fry in the mouth. The eggs are small.

G. B. Howes, "Notes on the Gular Brood-Pouch of *Rhinoderma darwini,"* *P. Zool. Soc.,* London, 1888, pp. 231-237. CUTANEOUS INCUBATION 133 period of incubation as during that of hibernation; but Howes found the small intestine normal and full of food-material in an assimilable condition, the large intestine fully charged with excreta, and the stomach distended with small beetles and diptera; and he adds that the alimentary viscera in general were those of a healthy animal in full diet. Howes thought that Espada was mistaken, but it seems possible that both conditions, hunger diet and full diet, may occur.

In contrast with the' foregoing examples of buccal incubation on the part of the male, we may quote cases of cutaneous incubation on the part of the female, as also in the male, both in fishes and batrachians. In the Lophobranchii or Pipe-fishes the cutaneous incubation of the eggs by the male attains a high degree of perfection within the family Syngnathidae; in the allied family Solenostomidae the ventral fins (absent in the Syngnathidae) are enlarged and combine together to form a brood-chamber, within which the eggs are borne upon cutaneous discs, but in this case the female performs the parental office. In the Siluroid genus *Aspredo,* which occurs in Guiana, Dr Giinther described the remarkable mode in which the female takes care of her ova, carrying them, after oviposition, attached to the spongy integument of the belly, as the Surinam toad *Pipa* carries her ova on the back. But a closer analogy than the Surinam toad is afforded by a Ceylon frog *Rhacophorus (Polypedates) reticulatus* as described by Giinther. Here the ova, about twenty in number, were found attached to the abdomen of the female, and when detached they adhered firmly together so as to form a flat disc. In the European Midwife toad, *Alytes obstetricans,* the mode of nursing is analogous to that of *Rhacophorus reticulatus,* except that in *Alytes* it is the male that takes care of the spawn.

In illustration of the widespread nature of the phenomenon of convergence may be mentioned a case of brood-nursing on the part of some insects. The family of amphibious water-bugs, Belostomatidae, is noted for the possession of the habit of carrying the eggs in the form of a disc cemented upon the back of the male, to which they are attached by the female. A species of this family where the habit can be observed with comparative ease is *Spharodema rusticum* Fabr., which occurs in the tanks of Ceylon amongst the weeds at the margin. The eggs remain on the back until the young hatch out into the water.

Amongst fresh-water fishes many cases of convergence are found in respect of the manner in which they prepare their nests and deposit their eggs. One pair of examples will suffice, *Ann. Nat. Hist.,* May, 1876, p. 379. *Cf.* W. L. Distant, "Rhynchota," *vol* iii. , *Fauna Brit. IncL,* 1906, p. 34. FLOATING EGGS 135 namely, the Indian murral, *Ophiocephalus striates,* as compared with the American bowfin, *Amia calva,* species which are far enough apart in the systematic scale, the former a Teleostean, the latter a Ganoid. Both make circular clearings in the shallow water of lakes or irrigation tanks, biting away the surrounding weeds; and in both cases the male parent tends the

nest, lying in wait in special runways. But whereas the eggs of *Amia* are strewn over the bottom of the nest, those of the murral float in a single layer at the surface, in contact with one another, but not adhering together. This exceptional behaviour of the eggs of a fresh-water fish is shared by those of another species of the same genus, *Ophiocephalus punctatus.*

These floating eggs of *Ophiocephalus* owe their buoyancy to the presence of a single large oilglobule, which occupies the greater part of the bulk of the ovum and is immersed in the ambercoloured yolk adjacent to the uppermost pole of the *egg.* The eggs thus come to lie immediately below the surface film of water, exposed to the quickening influence of air and sun, and protected thereby from the attacks of fungi, to which they are extremely liable as soon as the conditions of existence fall below a certain A. Willey, " Observations on the Nests, Eggs, and Larvae of *O. stria/us,"* *Spolia Zeylanica,* vol. vi., 1909 (1910), pp. 108-123. The comparison with *Amia* is based on the description given by Professor Bashford Dean.

optimum. For three days after hatching the larvae remain at the surface, floating on one side with yolk-sac well up. Before hatching, the body of the embryo encircles about two-thirds of the equatorial region of the yolk like a belt; the tail then twitches, the vitelline membrane is ruptured, and the larva with its yolk-sac is set free.

The floating eggs of these tropical fresh-water fishes are not comparable with the hyaline pelagic eggs of many marine fishes because they do not move from the nest; their buoyancy is part of the method of nidification and brooding, not a means of dispersal. I do not know any other instances of eggs of fresh-water fishes floating at the surface of the water by their own buoyancy; but the same advantages—proximity to atmospheric air and to sunlight—are secured in other ways, as by attachment to aquatic plants, or by deposition in very shallow water, or by special methods of nidification, as in the floating nests of *Gymnarchus* or the foam nests of *Sar-*

codaces, which were described by the late J. S. Budgett. There would seem, however, to be points of closer comparison between the eggs of the murral and those of some marine fishes, namely, the weevers (Trachinidae), according to the observations of J. Boeke (1903). These eggs are maintained *Cf.* The Budgett Memorial Volume, edited by J. Graham Kerr, Cambridge Univ. Press, 1907. YOLK-SACS 137 at the surface of the sea by means of a single large oil-globule; four or five days after oviposition the embryos are hatched; four or five days after hatching the yolk has become absorbed. The buoyancy of the yolk-sac causes the larvae to float helplessly for some time after hatching, with the yolk-sac uppermost.

The accumulation of yolk in eggs, or the lecithality of the ovum, also offers numerous examples of convergence as between cartilaginous fishes, bony fishes, and sauropsida (birds and reptiles) as well as amongst invertebrate animals. The large yolk-sacs of *Arius* and of *Gymnarchus* have no genetic relation to each other nor to those of sharks and rays. The yolk-sac of cephalopod molluscs is a structure *sui generis,* and it is particularly noteworthy that the most ancient existing genus, *Nautilus,* has the most macrolecithal egg of all whose eggs are known. CHAPTER IX

The Ways Of Breathing (respiratory Convergence)

The factors which combine to produce a structural or organic unit in the animal body which will be fixed—hy inheritance are inconceivably complex. Nevertheless, we have seen that essentially the same combination can be repeated independently in different cases. The present state of knowledge justifies the provisional assertion that the higher combination which leads to the establishment of an animal form possessing the essential component elements of a definite morphological type, cannot be repeated. The theory of convergence is therefore not calculated to precipitate us into morphological chaos, howsoever startling its manifestations may be.

A great deal might be written upon the large subject of respiratory convergence, but I will touch upon it briefly. Respiration is one of the primary properties of living matter, and the general principle which governs the mechanism of respiration, namely, the diffusion of gases (oxygen and carbon dioxide) through moist 138 MECHANISM OF RESPIRATION 139 membranes or across moist surfaceevis--ommon to all animals arid even to plants as.jwelljiut the special mechanism of respiration exhibits great phyletic diversity. There are four or five principal methods of breathing: (cutaneous) by the entire surface of the body, as with earthworms, leeches, and planarians; branchial, by specialised cutaneous processes called gills or branchiae, as with many marine Annelid worms, some leeches (Branchellion and Ozobranchus), molluscs, and Crustacea;(tracheal? 1 by air-tubes traversing the body and surrounding the viscera, as with insects and spiders; trematic, by gillclefts or visceral clefts piercing the body-wall and leading from the cavity of the pharynx or anterior part of the alimentary canal to the exterior; pulmonary, by lungs or air-chambers, as with pulmonate molluscs (Gastropods) and air-breathing vertebrates.

These different methods of respiration are not merely adaptations to the environment, but they are adaptations which keep pace with evolution independently of the environment. The superficial resemblance in shape of body, swimming movements, and burrowing habits, between the Annelid worm *Ophelia,* which breathes by simple filiform, cutaneous gills, and *Amphioxus,* which breathes by gill-clefts, has been remarked by Cav. Lo Bianco and by myself; they are often taken together in the same sandy bottom, in the Mediterranean and in the Indo-Pacific. The environment is identical; the adaptations are different according to their respective grades of evolution and lines of descent. Again, in many ways the Annelida are more highly organised than the Enteropneusta, though the latter possess gill-clefts.

An equal degree of resemblance based on convergence between members of distinct though allied families is that of the Jumping Blenny, *Salarias,* and the Jumping Goby, *Periophthalmus.* These fishes habitually come out of the water, the former to lounge and skip about rocks, the latter upon mud and mangrove roots; they both have large goggle-eyes and both can leap about as a normal mode of progression out of water, while the jumping goby can also ricochet over the surface of the water. As described by Moseley and again by Hickson, *Periophthalmus* jumps both out of water and on the surface by means of the bent, muscular, pectoral fins, of course assisted by the tail. *Salarias,* which is common on certain parts of the coast of Ceylon, performs surprising leaps by the action of its tail, which is kept curved when on the ground ready for a spring. Any one familiar with *Periophthalmus,* which is one of the everyday sights in suitable localities in the Eastern Tropics, H. N. Moseley," Notes by a Naturalist on H. M.S. *Challenger?* second edit. London, 1892.

S. J. Hickson, "A Naturalist in North Celebes." London, 1889. AIR-BREATHING FISHES 141 would be certain to mistake *Salarias* for it unless otherwise instructed. When out of water the opercular membrane is kept closely pressed against the body behind the gill-opening, so that the gill-cavity is temporarily converted into a virtual lung-chamber.

Other fishes which can progress out of water on suitable ground without falling on to one side are *Anabas, Clarias, Saccobranchus, Ophiocephalus,* and others. These may all be designated walking fishes. *Anabas* helps itself along by means of its opercular spines, *Clarias* and *Saccobranchus* by their pectoral spines, *Ophiocephalus* by movements of its flattened head, assisted by flexions of body and tail. All of these fishes can and must breathe air by means of special growths or diverticula connected with the upper division of the gill-cavity above the gill-clefts. *Clarias* and *Saccobranchus* are both Siluroids, but the corallike dendritic appendages in the suprapharyngeal chambers in *Clarias* are much more like the lamelliform labyrinthine organs in *Anabas*

than the diverticula of *Saccobranchus.* If these airbreathing Teleostean fishes are prevented from reaching the surface in order to take the air, they become drowned; and this habitual aropneustic function of the accessory branchial organs was, when first demonstrated, regarded by Professor Huxley as a great fact. *Saccobranchus* will live Rev. Barcroft Boake, "On the Air-Breathing Fish of Ceylon," *Journ. Ceylon Branch Roy. Asiat. Soc,* iv., 1867-1870.

longer out of water than it will when kept in water and deprived of access to the surface, but it cannot withstand desiccation, nor will it voluntarily leave the water when the latter is polluted; if its excursions to the surface are not sufficient to counteract the poisonous effects of the gaseous exhalations from the muddy bottom of a stagnant pool, it will perish miserably, sometimes coincidently with its last gulp of air, as I have witnessed.

The above-named fishes are amphipneustic without being amphibious, and in this respect are comparable, by way of convergence, with the fresh-water pulmonate Mollusca (Limnaeidae) and with the Dipnoan fishes or Dipnoi; whilst the latter are comparable, by way of homology, with the Amphibia. The respiratory movements of the legless batrachian, *Ichthyophis,* which, with the loss of appendages, has still retained many primitive features, involve the entire branchial or pharyngeal region including the throat, rapid contractions shimmering over from the ventral to the dorsal surface, while the nasal orifices are kept perpetually open. The original branchial region is clearly marked off like a collar from the rest of the body during life (Fig. 12), and the impression conveyed, which is in accordance with its known anatomical structure, is *Cf.* the elaborate monograph by Drs P. and F. Sarasin. The incubation of its eggs, the parent coiling round the egg-clump, resembles that of a Python.

ICHTHYOPHIS 143 that while the essential organs of respiration have changed from gill-clefts to lungs, the muscular and skeletal mechanism of respiration has remained practically unchanged. It may be added that *Ichthyophis* is a good swimmer but tries to get out of water as soon as possible, creeping with difficulty on a free surface by serpentine jerks, but moving easily through narrow crevices where its contact requirements *(i.e.,* stereotropism) are satisfied. Similar observations with regard to the respiratory movements have been made by my friend Professor Graham Kerr *(in litt.)* on the Dipnoan fish *Lepidosiren* Fig. 12. Head and fore-body of *Ichthyophisglutinosus* from above, to show the collar-like respiratory region. At the sides of the head in front of the eyes is the pair of peculiar retractile tentacles.

The fact that in the course of the substitution of lungs for gills the respiratory movements For a discussion of the nerve-supply *see* J. Graham Kerr, "Note on Swim-Bladder and Lungs," *Proc. Roy. Physical Soc.* Edinburgh, vol. xvii. , 1908, pp. 170-174.

are continued without interruption from the one to the other system, shows how the transition could be effected, but it does not, in my opinion, necessarily support Spengel's and Goette's theory of the origin of vertebrate lungs and air-bladders from gill-pouches. This is an interesting theory, and adds weight to the conception of the gillcleft as an autonomous "morphon," but there are difficulties in the way of its acceptance. In the first place, from the analogy of hydrostatic organs in other phyla, it does not seem necessary to invent a factitious explanation of the air-bladder as a gill-pouch derivative; the accumulation of air or gas in air-chambers is a widely distributed phenomenon, and in some fishes *(e.g.,* the Globe Fishes) the oesophagus itself can be converted into an air-chamber at the will of the animal.

There seems to be no particular difficulty in supposing that the air-bladder arose as a single or paired diverticulum of the fore-gut for the storage of air; and whether the first function was respiratory or hydrostatic or both, is another question. Spengel lays great stress upon the J. W. Spengel, " Ueber Schwimmblasen, Lungen und Kiementaschen der Wirbelthiere," *Zool. Jahrb. Suppl.,*

1904, pp. 727-749. In this paper the term "morphon" is suggested; it means a morphological unit or element.

Facts in support of the view that the original function of the air-bladder was respiratory were brought forward in a paper by Charles Morris on " The Origin of Lungs, a Chapter in Evolution," in *The American Naturalist,* vol. xxvi., 1892, pp. 975-986. This opinion is tentatively supported in principle by Hubrecht *(Joc. at.,* 1908), who refers to Assheton's paper on *"Gymnarchus"* in the Budgett Memorial Volume. MEGALOPS 145 fact that the arteries which supply the lungs of Dipnoi and the air-bladder of some other fishes (e.g., *Polypterus)* and the lungs of all air-breathing vertebrates from the Amphibia onwards, arise as branches of the fourth afferent branchial arteries. But Burne has shown that the accessory branchial diverticula or air-pouches of *Saccobranchus,* which penetrate the body musculature throughout the greater part of the length of the trunk from the gill-cavity to the tail, lying above the transverse processes on either side of the vertebral column, are also vascularised from the fourth afferent branchial artery on each side; but these airpouches co-exist with a true air-bladder. We have, in fact, in this case a very delicate example of vascular convergence.

The air-bladder of the estuarine Clupeoid fish *Megalops cyprinoides,* common in Ceylon, is provided on its inner surface with an abundance of spongy, vascular, alveolar proliferations which are especially dense just behind the large orifice by which it communicates directly, without the intermediation of a pneumatic duct, with the oesophagus immediately behind the gill-clefts dorsally; it is not vascularised from the branchial arches, but this species can live for a long time after capture, an uncommon feature in the R. H. Burne, " On the Aortic Arch System of *Saccobranchus fossilis,"* *Journ. Linn. Soc Zool.,* xxv., 1894, pp. 48-55.

herring family and contrary to the experience of the common herring.

The Siluroid fish *Arius falcarius,* of

which mention has been made above, exhibits great viability out of water. A large female, 14 inches long, which had been caught by a hook but had not been injured, lived for nearly five hours out of water, breathing regularly by mouth and gills, without accessory structures, closing the gill-cavity behind by the opercular membrane. After it had been out of water for about an hour I counted 80 buccal respirations to the minute, the opercular membrane beating time with the mouth but remaining quite closed behind. After two hours there were 70 respirations to the minute; and after three hours 60 feebler respirations, the opercular membrane now commencing to gape behind. At the end of the experiment the heart was removed and continued beating outside the body. This example shows that the phenomenon of viability out of water is something apart from the possession of accessory branchial organs.

Another Siluroid fish, *Plotosus canius,* exhibits similar viability, living from early morning until afternoon (over six hours) out of water, the gills remaining quite fresh to the end. In this case periodical expirations took place through the gill-opening; every now and then the opercular membrane was raised several times in succession, PLOTOSUS 147 and this was followed by a number of buccal inspirations without the gill-covers being reflected. The raising of the gill-covers coincides with the taking of a deep breath. I counted first 32 inspirations and 13 expirations in a minute, then 32 inspirations to 10 expirations; a third counting gave 30 and 11, a fourth 29 and 12. The expirations were not evenly distributed, sometimes 5 or 6 occurring together. These observations show the great physiological importance of the opercular membrane whose systematic worth is sometimes regarded as *nil.*

The typical Molluscan gill was named the ctenidium by Lankester in order to fix its morphological independence and to distinguish it from other gills of invertebrates such as the Annelid parapodial gill, the Crustacean arthropodial gill, the Limuloid gill-book, and others, as well as from secondary Molluscan pallial gills, as in the Prosobranchiate genus *Patella* (limpet) and in the Opisthobranchiate genera *Phyllidia* and *Pleurophyllidia*. Thus the organs of respiration which take the form of cutaneous gills are not homologous throughout; in other words, they are not monophyletic but polyphyletic in nature and origin; but the particular structure known as the ctenidium with which a special sensory apparatus, the osphradium and its nervesupply, is associated, is homologous throughout Zoological Articles *(Encyc. Brit.)*, Edinburgh, 1891.

the Molluscan phylum, that is to say, the ctenidium is monophyletic.

√ The spirally thickened air-tubes or tracheae of Myriopods, Insects, and Spiders bear so close a correspondence in structure and function, ramifying through the body like blood-vessels, but effecting the circulation of air instead of blood, that all the air-breathing Arthropods were formerly classed together as Tracheata in contradistinction to the aquatic Arthropods which were called Branchiata.

For more than a quarter of a century it has been recognised that the Tracheate Arthropods could not be reduced to a common standard, and it has also come to be realised that the tracheae of Insects and Arachnids have had separate origins, and are therefore different morphologically though similar histologically and physiologically.

This fundamental example of tracheal convergence is rendered more remarkable by the fact that even within the limits of the Arachnoid subphylum, the tracheae have had at least a twofold origin, namely, from lung-books and from ectodermal tendons; so that "similarity of structure in the fully developed tracheae does not mean similarity of origin " Purcell. Purcell has shown that the tendinal or medial tracheal trunks in Dipneumonous spiders are equivalent in their entirety to metamorphosed entapophyses (ectodermal tendons); the lateral tracheal trunks, on TRACHEAL CONVERGENCE 149 the contrary, are serially homologous with the pulmonary

sacs of the preceding somite, and actually homologous with the second pair of pulmonary sacs in Tetrapneumonous spiders.

Purcell affirms that the arguments in favour of the branchial origin of the lung-books of spiders, advocated by Lankester in 1881, appear overwhelming. An interesting analogy may therefore be drawn between the Pulmonate Arachnida and the Pulmonate Mollusca, where a lungchamber has likewise been substituted for a gill-chamber; and just as in Arachnida, according to Pocock (1893), there is reason to believe that tracheal tubes have replaced lung-books at least twice, namely, in the Dipneumones and in the Pseudoscorpiones; so in the Land Mollusca a pulmonary chamber has twice replaced a gillchamber, namely, in the Land Operculates, which belong to the order Prosobranchiata, and in the inoperculate Pulmonata, which are related to the Opisthobranchiata.

The internal trachea? (of cutaneous origin) are not homologous throughout the Arthropod phylum—they are polyphyletic like the external cutaneous branchiae of soft-bodied invertebrates.

Now with regard to the trematic mode of aquatic respiration, or breathing by means of gill-clefts, the question naturally arises whether W. F. Purcell, "Development and Origin of the Respiratory Organs in Araneae," *Quart. Journ. Micr. Sc,* vol. liv., 1909, pp. I-no; contains full bibliography.

the latter are another generalised form of respiratory organ which may have arisen *de novo* in different divisions of the animal kingdom, or whether gill-clefts are not rather a specialised formation, homologous throughout, like the Molluscan ctenidium. The analogies of the cutaneous branchiae and tracheae render the question a legitimate one for discussion and an extremely difficult one to settle. Many zoologists, of whom I happen to be one, think that the gill-cleft is a monophyletic structure, and in order to give effect to this point of view I suggested, as a *memoria technica,* the phylogenetic term Branchiotrema, to include all animals possessing gill-clefts

at any period of their life-history.

The extraordinary persistence of gill-clefts and gill-pouches in the embryos of the higher lung-breathing vertebrates, the constancy of their innervation in all Craniate vertebrates, and the combination of structures which accompany them in all Chordates, speak for their homogeneity. Whilst we may admit that the general homology of gill-clefts' is open to question, we must at the same time assert that the burden of proof to the *Cf*. A. Willey, "Enteropneusta from the South Pacific," *Zoological Results,* part iii., Cambridge, 1899, pp. 223-334. *See* also R. C. Punnett's memoir on the Enteropneusta from the Maldive and Laccadive Islands in Stanley Gardiner's "Fauna and Flora of the Maldive and Laccadive Islands," 1904-1905.

GILL-CLEFTS 151 contrary rests with those who deny it. Up to the present there has been no brilliant demonstration of the diphyletic origin of gill-clefts. The assumed homology between the gill-clefts of the Enteropneusta and those of Amphioxus has been doubted because their histological composition is not identical; but we know now that histological identity is no safer guide to morphology than is anatomical identity. This is where the matter rests at present with regard to trematic respiration. The differences between the gill-clefts of the Enteropneusta where the tongue-bar is the principal component, and the gill-clefts of Amphioxus where the tongue-bar is a secondary component, are such as one would be prepared to find in allied groups which present unequal grades of organisation.

We have already mentioned several examples of convergent pulmonate respiration, and it only remains to be added, for the sake of completeness, that the lungs of the higher vertebrates are acknowledged, on grounds of comparative anatomy, to be homologous with the air-bladder of Teleostean fishes in spite of differences in the vascularisation and topography of these organs.

According to Owen (Preface to Hunter's *Animal Oeconomy,* 1837), Harvey was the first to compare the abdominal air-sacs of the bird with those of reptiles and fishes; and in this he was followed by John Hunter, who discovered the

"air-cells" in the bones and muscular interstices of birds in 1774, simultaneously with Camper. The abdominal air-sacs of birds are appendages of the lungs, and although there exists a general homology between lungs and the air-sac of fishes, there is no special homology between the abdominal extensions of the lungs in birds and the latter.

CHAPTER X

Convergence In Minute Structure
(histogenetic Convergence)

In the preceding chapter we have seen that histogenetic convergence gives no clue to affinity, and that histogenetic divergence is no proof of want of affinity. We may now go further than this and add that where we do find actual histological identity, as between members of different phyla, it seems certain that we are in the presence of true convergence in the sense in which that term is employed here; and, in the light of facts which are now available, it even begins to appear strange, although only a matter of a few years or months ago, that histological identity should ever have been insisted upon as a criterion of homology except within well-defined limits.

To my thinking, one of the most remarkable examples of histogenetic convergence is that of the excretory organs of Amphioxus as compared with those of certain Annelid worms. The excretory tubules of Amphioxus were discovered independently by Weiss and Boveri in 1890 and were described in detail by the latter in 1892. Attached in clusters to the walls of the tubules Boveri found long pinshaped cells, which he called "Fadenzellen" (thread-cells), projecting into the dorsal coelom. They appeared to consist of a small roundish cell-body mounted upon a long thread-like stalk which was inserted into the tubule. Ten years later Goodrich, who had been making some notable discoveries in regard to the structure of the nephridia of Polychaete worms, turned his attention to the tubules of Amphioxus and promptly

discovered that Boveri's thread-cells are identical with the solenocytes which he had found in Polychaeta.

Goodrich showed that Boveri's thread-like stalk is really a slender hollow tube of great length, carrying the cell-body floating in the coelom, or adhering to the adjacent walls of the coelom, at its distal end, and opening into the renal tubule at the proximal end. "A long flagellum attached at its base to the cell placed at the end of the tube works rapidly down the tube and far into the excretory canal." Goodrich observes that the excretory organs of Amphioxus and the nephridia of *Phyllodoce* are in all essentials identical, and he adds that "if two such excretory organs as the solenocyte-bearing nephridia of *Phyllodoce,* and the solenocyte-bearing kidneys E. S. Goodrich, "On the Structure of the Excretory Organs of Amphioxus," Part i., *Quart. Jour. Micr. Sc.,* vol. xlv., 1902, pp493-Soi; Part ii. *Ibid.* vol. liv., 1909, pp. 185-205.

SOLENOCYTES 155 of Amphioxus could be shown to have been independently evolved, we should have to give up structural resemblance as a guide to homology." He says in a footnote that the only case which seems to him at all comparable is that of the nematocysts in Coelenterates, Planarians, and Molluscs. To this case we may add the myoepithelial cells in Coelenterates, Nematodes, and Tunicata; and, as Goodrich admits, the flame-cells of flatworms, Rotifers, and Polyzoa (Entoprocta) are probably of the same nature as his solenocytes.

I venture to interpret Goodrich's discovery as a brilliant demonstration of histogenetic convergence and submit the following explanation, basing the argument on personal conviction, on an appeal to known facts, and on certain general considerations:—

Just as various offices are constituent parts of the body politic, so various organs are constituent parts of the animal economy. Pharynx, cesophagus, crop, gizzard, stomach, liver and other diverticula, intestine and rectum, are constituent parts of the digestive tract of a

coelomate animal and are likely to appear when called into requisition by the necessities of adaptation and evolution; and equally likely to disappear when not specially required. I may refer here to the remarkably simple digestive tract of the Scombresocidae (e.g., *Belone),* where the oesophagus is suppressed, the outward differentiation of the stomach is lacking, and there is no pylorus and no pyloric cceca. So again, continuing our analysis, we find that flame-cells or solenocytes, nematocysts, myoepithelial cells, spicule-forming cells, ganglion cells, pigment cells, striated muscle cells, etc., may be regarded as belonging to the category or repertory of the primary constituent elements of animal tissues, and will appear when required to fit in with a special set of physiological conditions. Let us imagine a limited number of primary physiological conditions of excretion. Some or all of these conditions will recur independently in each of the phyla of the animal kingdom. To meet them, the necessary cellular elements, till then held in abeyance, will be forthcoming.

Bewildering as may be the striking identity which Goodrich has established between the solenocytes of Amphioxus and of Polychaetes, it is perhaps not more remarkable in principle than other cases of identical anatomical differentiation, some of which have been referred to in the preceding chapters.

As might have been expected, this case of nephridial convergence has been hailed with delight by Dr Gaskell, who looks upon it as an acceptable confirmation of his deductions. I may be permitted to make the following quotation from his book, whilst at the same time SOLENOCYTES 157 strongly recommending the reader, if he has not done so already, to refer to the original volume, which is a very remarkable document of research. The citation will serve to illustrate Dr Gaskell's point of view in this matter, and I make no further comment upon it, relying upon what has gone before—except to point out that it is not quite correct to say that the Polychaeta as a whole are the highest forms of Annelida. It is precisely among the

Polychaeta that the nervous system is often in contact with the epidermis, and it is here that the cerebral ganglion retains its primitive position in the prostomium.

This is what he says:—" It is to me most interesting to find that the very group of Annelids, the Polychata, which possess solenocytes so remarkably resembling those _pf the excretory organs of Amphioxus, are the highest and most developed of all the Annelida. I have argued throughout that the law of evolution consists in the origination of successive forms from the dominant group then alive, dominance signifying the highest type of brainpower achieved up to that time." The ways of evolution are obscure and peculiar; logically one would think that they ought to keep pace with the increase of brain-power; naturally W. H. Gaskell, "The Origin of Vertebrates," London, 1908, see p. 395. we find that the increase of brain-power is merely an incident in evolution.

It will be appropriate at this point to consider another example of what I hold to be histogenetic convergence as between the lateral senseorgans of the Polychaete family of the Capitellidae, the abdominal sense-organs of Lamellibranchiate Molluscs, and the lateral line sense-organs of Vertebrates, thus involving three distinct phyla. The lateral organs of Capitellida e are absolutely comparable to the lateral line organs of Vertebrata, but only by way of convergence, not by way of homology.

Let us first look at the abdominal sense-organs of the bivalve molluscs, about which I am able to speak with some authority inasmuch as, in one instance, namely, that of the Windowpane Oyster, Placuna placenta, I have found the true unpaired abdominal sense-organ which had been overlooked by previous investigators. The story of our knowledge of these sense-organs is interesting. The year 1881 saw a considerable advance in the morphology of the Mollusca in consequence of the publication of Spengel's paper on their so-called olfactory organs, subsequently called the osphradia by Lankester, and on the nervous system. In dealing with

the Lamellibranchiata he was at first at a loss where to look for them, but, thanks to a lucky chance (" einem gliicklichen Zufalle "), on opening an Arca noce he saw at once, ABDOMINAL SENSE-OR-GANS 159 between the hinder end of the foot and the vent, a transverse, undulating line of greenish-brown pigment interrupted in the middle line by a narrow interval. That line proved to mark the position of the pigmented sense-organs for which he was searching. In the figure which he gave to elucidate the topography of these organs, another pair of organs, on either side of the vent, was indicated with great distinctness, although no reference was made to them in the text. These latter organs were, eight years later, shown by J. Thiele to represent a pair of abdominal sensory papillae having a highly characteristic structure and innervated by a fine nerve proceeding backwards on each side from the visceral ganglion.

When examined in toto in a fresh preparation the abdominal sense-organs are chiefly characterised by the possession of a dense coating of long, motionless, stiff cilia or sense-hairs. In transverse section these cilia are seen to be carried by a very high epithelium containing numerous basal nuclei at different levels, an intermediate layer of nuclei at one level, and a clear peripheral zone. Thiele described the organs in a number of bivalves, including a species of scallop, Pecten varius, where he found a sensory ridge on the right side only, there being no corresponding ridge on the left side Zeitschr. wiss. ZOOL, xlviii., 1889, pp. 47-59. in this species. Similar relations have been described by Dakin in another species of scallop, Pecten maximus, and the unpaired condition of the organ is obviously a character of the genus Pecten.

In the Oriental disc-shaped bivalve, Placuna placenta, belonging to the family Anomiidae, only one sensory abdominal ridge occurs. It is defined by the presence of brown pigment, and is placed upon the edge of an adrectal ligament or cutaneous fold which unites the rectal complex with the right mantle

lobe at about the level of the posterior insertion of the suspensory ligament of the right ctenidium. The pallial circulation of Placuna is characterised by the presence of a pair of ascending pallial vessels, which arise from the circumpallial arteries at the posteroventral border of each mantle lobe and pass obliquely upwards towards the posterior end of the suprabranchial region. On approaching the latter their walls are usually inflated, after the valves have been separated, to form an elongated oblong or elliptical body which is non-contractile. I do not know the precise significance of this congestion of the walls of the ascending pallial vessels of Placuna, but it concerns the vascular system and has nothing to do with the adrectal sensory organ.

The abdominal sense-organ of Placuna con Memoir on Pecten. Liverpool, 1909.

SENSE-ORGAN OF PLACUNA 161 forms in its general histological structure to those previously described in other Lamellibranchs, and I have had the opportunity of comparing it in section with the paired, whitish, adrectal, semilunar organs of Arca rhombea, a species which occurs in the same localities as Placuna in the back-waters of the eastern province of Ceylon, near Trincomalee. Transverse sections of the sense-organ in Placuna, stained with alum carmine, show externally the dense layer of perfectly preserved, stiff, sensory cilia, exceeding in length the height of the sensory epithelium. At their bases they perforate the stout, cuticular membrane, which presents a double contour. Below the cuticle there follows an outer prismatic layer, then a middle layer of evenly placed elliptical, nuclear bodies representing the layer of spindles; thirdly, an inner fibrillar layer, and finally a basal plexus of nuclear bodies adjoining the basement membrane which separates the epithelium from the gelatinous conjunctive tissue upon which it rests.

Thiele emphasised the extraordinary resemblance between the epithelium of the Molluscan abdominal organs and the Annelid lateral organs as described by Eisig in the Capitellidae; and satisfied himself by actual comparison of preparations that in fact the similarity is very close.

Recently another pair of sense-organs, histologically resembling the abdominal sense-organs though quite different topographically, has been described by M. Stenta in a Protobranchiate bivalve mollusc. These are the marginal pallial sense-organs of *Leda commutata* (Nuculidae) which occur right and left at the anterior junction of the right and left mantle lobes, lying in a crypt on each side between the inner and middle folds of the pallial margin. If any one ventured to argue that the posterior adrectal or abdominal organs of Lamellibranchiata might be related by way of homology to the segmental abdominal organs of Capitellidae, the same argument could not be applied to the anterior pallial organs of *Leda,* although all these structures apparently belong to one physiological category, namely, rheostatic organs. We may confidently conclude that they are related to each other only by way of sensory convergence. In this connection we may take note of the well-known case of retinal convergence between the pallial eyes of the scallop and the cerebral eyes of vertebrates.

Eisig treated the lateral sense-organs of Capi tellidai under two categories — thoracic organs appearing in surface view as open pores; and abdominal organs, appearing as retractile knobs or elevations, the distal extremity of which is beset with stiff sense-hairs radiating in all directions.

Mario Stenta, "Ober ein neues Mantelrandorgan bei *Leda commutata? Zool. Anz.,* xxxv., 1909, pp. 154-157. Hugo Eisig," Die Capitelliden." "Fauna und Flora des Golfes von Neapel." Berlin, 1887. SENSE-ORGANS OF Capitellidje 163

These sense-organs were closely compared by Eisig with the lateral line sense-organs of aquatic vertebrates (fishes and batrachians), the function of which is partly equilibrating and partly the perception of currents and wave-movements. The most remarkable histological resemblance is manifested between the lateral sense-organs of the Capitellidae and the lateral line sense-organs of Vertebrates. In both cases the essential organs consist of small, solid, roundish, epidermal buds, from which fine stiff sense-hairs project freely into the surrounding medium; and the resemblance is further enhanced by their segmental arrangement. The correspondence could hardly be greater, the convergence could hardly be closer, the homology could not be more remote than infinity.

Within the limits of the order of Polychaeta, Eisig has established the true homology between the lateral sense-organs of Capitellidae and the dorsal cirri of neural parapodia such as occur in the family Glyceridae. Through this family it is made clear that the lateral organs are homologous with the dorsal cirri of Polychaeta as a whole.

Most morphological arguments work both ways, and it is not surprising that after having established the homology between the endostyle of Amphioxus and the Ascidians and the thyroid gland of Ammocoetes, the larval form of the lamprey, Dohrn, committed to the Annelid Theory of vertebrate descent, should have concluded that the endostyle was derived by descent with simplification from the more elaborate organ in Ammocoetes, in which opinion he has been supported by Gaskell. Regressive convergence *by* reduction and loss of parts is indeed a very common phenomenon, expressive of the levelling effects of degeneration, *e.g.,* the loss of limbs in snakes, some lizards, some batrachians, and some fishes; compare also the effects of sedentary and parasitic habits. In less obvious cases this principle has to be applied with the utmost circumspection.

For Gaskell's views on the homology which he supposes to exist between the thyroid gland of Ammocoetes and the uterus of the scorpion, the reader should consult the work quoted above. For my present purpose the following passage will suffice *op. cit.,* p. 205):—" The resemblance between the structure of the thyroid of Ammocoetes and the uterus of the scorpion is most striking, except in two respects, viz., the nature of the lining of the non-glandular part of the cavity—in the one case ciliated, in the other chitinous—and the place of exit of the cavity, the thyroid of Ammocoetes opening into the respiratory chamber, while the uterus of Scorpio opens direct to the exterior." It may be added by way of explanation that the supposed homology MESOSOMA 165 is founded, in the first instance, upon the mutual topographical proximity of the respiratory apparatus, and of the terminal portion of the genital apparatus in the scorpion group and in Limulus the King Crab, and the relations of these organs to the segments of the mesosoma.

It is not easy to deal with this comparison in a satisfactory manner. It seems to be somewhat gratuitous and to proceed from a fallacious assumption of community of regional differentiation. We have seen in several instances that identity of structure and function may go for nothing in determining homology, and that the same identity has no relation to topography. If one chooses to compare the respiratory region of the scorpion or of Limulus with that of Ammocoetes, and to dub it mesosoma in both cases, all sorts of curious sequences will be encountered. Without a preconceived bias, such as Dr Gaskell does not_ conceal, namely, in respect of his ideas upon dominance and_ brain-power, one would not consider the two regions comparable morphologically. It is a very good thing to have a guiding idea in morphology and to follow it out, but at the best it can only lead to a subjective conclusion. There is no necessity to confound such a conclusion with the truth, and this is all we can ask, since the reconciliation of the truth with one's individual views is not a matter which can be settled within a generation. At the same time it would seem proper to insist here that in the face of an assertive logical system which can only be combated at the expense of infinite weariness and vexation, the best and only course is to hold fast to what one adopts intuitively as first principles; and, with regard to the special case before us, to regard the gill-cleft as an autonomous morphon and the Limuloid gill-book, with its derivative the lung-book of Arachnida, as another autonomous morphon, having nothing in common except their function.

The histological resemblance between the glandular part of the thyroid of Ammocoetes and the glandular part of the uterus of the scorpion may be regarded as a case of glandular convergence, and as such it possesses a peculiar interest of its own.

Now if we reject the Limuloid Theory of Vertebrate descent, why should we accept as normal the theory of the Arachnoid affinities of Limulus? The answer in brief is that the normal morphology of Arachnoids and of Vertebrates respects phyletic boundaries; and that the convergent morphology of these groups transcends those limits. Both are good so long as they are kept apart.

It would, of course, be possible to multiply examples of histological parallelism to an almost unlimited extent by comparing distantly related CYTOLOGY 167 forms and making extracts from published records. All animals are related together by the continuity of the germ-plasm; the remoter the relationship, the closer the convergence may be, and *vice versa*. An instance of nuclear convergence has been noted recently by Minchin. In the collar-cells of some calcareous sponges (Clathrinidae) he found that the nucleus occupies a position at the base of the cell, and the flagellum arises independently from a granule or blepharoplast situated at the surface of the cell in the centre of the area enclosed by the collar. In the Leucosoleniidae the nucleus occupies an apical position and the flagellum appears as a direct continuation of the pointed end of the nucleus.

Minchin quotes a parallelism to these alternative positions of the nucleus in the case of two species of *Mastigina* described by Goldschmidt (1907). Such a character, adds Minchin, in the case of sponges, can have but little importance in the struggle for existence, and yet in his opinion it indicates the deepest phylogenetic divergence in the pedigree of the calcareous sponges.

Cytological convergence, as between Metazoa and Protozoa, yields many points of instructive E. A. Minchin, "The Relation of the Flagellum to the Nucleus in the Collar-Cells of Calcareous Sponges." *Zool. Anz.,xxxv.,* 1909, p. 227.
comparison. The phenomena of intracellular digestion, phagocytosis, and wandering cells come under this category. An elaborate case is that of the pulsating, multinucleated chromatophores of eight-armed Cephalopoda. In Octopus, under certain conditions of excitement, the play of colour may be observed taking place with marvellous regularity and rapidity. Each chromatophore, as Chun has demonstrated, is a single disc-shaped cell with contractile processes radiating from the periphery; and these contractile processes originate from the cell-body in the same manner as the pseudopodia of a rhizopod Protozoan.
The preceding examples bear witness to the truth of the conclusion that convergence depends equally upon the unity of plan of composition of the body of animals, as indicated in the incidence of planes of symmetry, and upon the continuity of the system of functions from Protozoa to Metazoa.

Now, if we stop for a moment to enquire what is the bearing of all this, it may be said that I have failed in my purpose unless it has been made abundantly clear that the influence of convergence in evolution has been widespread, Carl Chun, " Uber dieNatur und die Entwicklung der Chromatophoren bei den Cephalopoden." *Verh. d. Deutschen Zool. Ges.,* 1902, pp. 162-182.
MORPHONS AND TROPISMS 169 deep-seated, and intimate, more so than is generally recognised. What may appear to be a brilliant discovery of morphological affinity may in reality be an equally brilliant demonstration of the no less important and interesting phenomenon of morphological convergencej the closer the identity, as between forms belonging to different phyla, the greater likelihood, or, as I should prefer to say,

the greater certainty that it is due to convergence.
What is known as homoplasy in morphology might be called homotaxis ihionomics In contrast with the phenomenon of change of Junction we have that of substitution of organs, as Kleinenberg expressed it, or change of morphon in Spengel's phraseology. Similarly, in contrast with the Tropism Theory we must have the Morphon Theory, and we must distinguish between primary or general morphons which are, with due reserves, the intrinsic property of all animals, and secondary or phyletic morphons which are the special characteristics of distinct groups. The relation of morphons to tropisms lies at the basis of all orthogenetic morphology and all convergent morphology. Under the one or the other heading all pertinent facts can be ranged, and none need be left out of the reckoning.

It will be observed that no attempt has been made in the foregoing pages to formulate any laws of orthogenesis and convergence. A greater assemblage of facts thanTiasTbeen marshalled here would be necessary, nothing short of a new cyclopaedia of anatomy and physiology, and probably the time is not yet ripe for that. Up to the present no other work jwith which I am acquainted has dealt with convergence_as a general and positive phenomenon of equal importance with orthogenesis or normal morphology, although isolated cases are referred to in most text-books of zoology and are exhibited in most natural history museums.

The fact that no laws of convergence are or even can be laid down now is one which is fraught with the greatest hope for the future of morphology; and the breaking down of the former landmarks of homology, such as histological structure and metameric repetition, except within narrow limits, offers a great opportunity for emancipation from the trammels of speculation. If we were to tabulate laws they would not be natural, but merely dogmatic, at the mercy of the first unbeliever. Hardly one universal criterion of strict homology can be mentioned which would pass muster in a critical examination. Then away with laws and away with criteria until they cease to obscure the facts as they are.

Hypotheses are one of the chief means of progress in morphology. Without them the advances which have been made during the past hundred years would not have been so considerable. If the hypothesis is constructed after the work is done or before it is completed, the work accomplished remains after the need for the hypothesis, which is either the best clue that one can give for the time being or the best guide that one can follow, has passed away. In morphology everything is important except the hypothesis, although practically nothing could be done without it, since it is often the only means available for digesting an accumulation of facts. It is something intangibly necessary, often quite wrong, always hopelessly incomplete, but ever ready to give way by substitution to another invisible vehicle. The progress of morphology depends upon the substitution of ideas rather than upon the promulgation of laws. The tree of life is polyphyletic, and the branches do not anastomose after their zigzag course has been set.

عمن الرحيم والصلاة والسلام على رسول الله

In the name of God, the Most Graci
Merciful, and prayers and peace
the Messenger of God.

God said in Surah Al-Baqara, Verse 185:

شَهْرُ رَمَضَانَ الَّذِي أُنزِلَ فِيهِ الْقُرْآنُ هُدًى لِّلنَّاسِ وَبَيِّنَاتٍ مِّنَ الْهُدَىٰ وَالْفُرْقَانِ فَمَن شَهِدَ مِنكُمُ الشَّهْرَ فَلْيَصُمْهُ وَمَن كَانَ مَرِيضًا أَوْ عَلَىٰ سَفَرٍ فَعِدَّةٌ مِّنْ أَيَّامٍ أُخَرَ يُرِيدُ اللَّهُ بِكُمُ الْيُسْرَ وَلَا يُرِيدُ بِكُمُ الْعُسْرَ وَلِتُكْمِلُوا الْعِدَّةَ وَلِتُكَبِّرُوا اللَّهَ عَلَىٰ مَا هَدَاكُمْ وَلَعَلَّكُمْ تَشْكُرُونَ

The month of Ramadan in which was revealed the Quran, a guidance for mankind and clear proofs for the guidance and the criterion (between right and wrong). So whoever of you sights (the crescent on the first night of) the month of Ramadan i.e. is present at his home), he must observe Saum (fasts) that month, and whoever is ill or on a journey, the same number [of days which one did not observe Saum (fasts) must e made up] from other days. Allah intends for you ease, and He does not want to make things difficult for you. He wants that you) must complete the same number (of days), nd that you must magnify Allah [i.e. to say Takbir (Allahu-Akbar; llah is the Most Great) on seeing the crescent of the months of Ramadan and Shawwal] for having guided you so that you may be grateful to Him.

① 1

Contents:

by Mohamed Alaoui 2020/1441 AH

Pillars of Islam

1. To testify that none is worthy of worship but Allaah and that Muhammad is the Messenger of Allaah.

2. To perform prayers.

3. To pay zakaah.

4. To fast the month of Ramadan.

5. To perform Hajj.

Islamic Months

1 Muharram		7 Rajab	
2 Safar		8 Sha'ban	
3 Rabi al-Awwal		9 Ramadan	
4 Rabi al-Thani		10 Shawwal	
5 Jumada al-Awwal		11 Dhul-Qa'dah	
6 Jumada al-Thani		12 Dhul-Hijjah	

What is the month of Ramadan?

Ramadan is the ninth month of the Islamic calendar. During the month of Ramadan, Muslim adults fast from sunrise to sunset except for the sick, traveler or young child.

The month of Ramadan is the best month of the year. It is the month in which God revealed the Noble Qur'an, God has imposed fasting in it, and the month has been given favors and virtues that are not the same, and fasting also has many benefits.

When does Ramadan start and when does it end?

The months in the Islamic calendar begin and end when the crescent is seen, the duration of one month is between 28 and 30 days, and there is no time in the year to determine when exactly begins or when it ends, it varies from year to year, the month of Ramadan may be this year in the spring, but After a few years it will be in the winter and after a few more years it will be in the fall and so on ..., and the month that precedes it is called Shaaban, and the month after that is named Shawwal.

The merits of Ramadan:

The month of fasting, the month of Laylat al-Qadr, the month of qiyam al-layl, the month of multiplication from the recitation of the Noble Qur'an, the month of emancipation from the fire, the month of multiplication of charity(Sadaqah), the month in which Umrah equals an argument with the Messenger, may God bless him and grant him peace.

The month of fasting

Fasting is the fourth pillar of Islam.

Fasting is for a Muslim to refrain from eating and drinking from sunrise to sunset.

God says in the quran: Surah Al-Baqara, Verse 183

يَا أَيُّهَا الَّذِينَ آمَنُوا كُتِبَ عَلَيْكُمُ الصِّيَامُ كَمَا كُتِبَ عَلَى الَّذِينَ مِن قَبْلِكُمْ لَعَلَّكُمْ تَتَّقُونَ

(O you who believe! Observing As-Saum (the fasting" is prescribed for you as it was prescribed for those "before you, that you may become Al-Muttaqun

⑧

DOOR IN PARADISE CALLED AL RAYYAN

In Paradise there is a door for the fasting person called Al Rayyan.

The doors of Heaven are opened

The doors of Heaven are opened,
the doors of fire closed and the demons
restricted.

Allah's Messenger (ﷺ) said

رَسُولَ اللَّهِ صلى الله عليه وسلم قَالَ "إِذَا جَاءَ رَمَضَانُ فُتِحَتْ أَبْوَابُ الْجَنَّةِ".

"When Ramadan begins, the gates of Paradise
are opened."

the last ten days of Ramadan

In the last ten days of Ramadan there will be a great night called the Night of Power, which is a night better than a thousand months, in which many angels descend, there is a surah in the Qur'an called Surat Al-Qadr

God Almighty says in Surat Al-Qadr:

بِسْمِ اللَّهِ الرَّحْمَنِ الرَّحِيمِ

إِنَّا أَنْزَلْنَاهُ فِي لَيْلَةِ الْقَدْرِ (1) وَمَا أَدْرَاكَ مَا لَيْلَةُ الْقَدْرِ (2) لَيْلَةُ الْقَدْرِ خَيْرٌ مِنْ أَلْفِ شَهْرٍ (3) تَنَزَّلُ الْمَلَائِكَةُ وَالرُّوحُ فِيهَا بِإِذْنِ رَبِّهِمْ مِنْ كُلِّ أَمْرٍ (4) سَلَامٌ هِيَ حَتَّى مَطْلَعِ الْفَجْرِ (5)

IN THE NAME OF ALLAH, THE BENEFICENT, THE MERCIFUL

"Indeed, We sent the Qur'an down during the Night of Decree.(1)

And what can make you know what is the Night of Decree?(2)

The Night of Decree is better than a thousand months.(3)

The angels and the Spirit descend therein by permission of their Lord for every matter.(4)

Peace it is until the emergence of dawn.(5)

Night prayers (Salat Qiyaam Al-layl)

A prayer that takes place at night after the evening prayer and before the dawn prayer, which is a prayer that is a great reward for God. A Muslim may perform an unlimited number of rak'ahs. It may be in the other days and months, but in Ramadan the reward is more than the rest of the months, so any work in the month of Ramadan has more reward than the other months.

He who performs this prayer has a great reward, and he who does not perform it has no sin, because it is not from the obligatory prayer.

> God Almighty forgive many Muslims
> every night of Ramadan

this is a penalty for them for their worship of Him and for carrying out what He asks of them.

The Prophet (ﷺ) said

«مَن قامَ ليلةَ القدرِ إيمانًا واحتِسابًا غُفِرَ لَهُ ما تقدَّمَ من ذنبِهِ»

"Whoever established prayers on the night of Qadr out of sincere faith and hoping for a reward from Allah, then all his previous sins will be forgiven; and whoever fasts in the month of Ramadan out of sincere faith, and hoping for a reward from Allah, then all his previous sins will be forgiven."

The month of reading of the Holy Quran

Reading the Qur'an is one of the greatest acts of worship and it has a great reward that motivates the Muslim to take advantage of Ramadan and read a lot of the Qur'an and searches for its interpretation and the purpose of the verses, and many Muslims read the entire Qur'an in the month of Ramadan, and whoever reads it all more than once.

The month of a lot of charity
(SADAKAH)

Charity has several meanings, including giving people in need what they need, such as money, food, clothing, etc. .... And charity may be with other actions such as a smile while meeting people, also if in some way or street something hurts pedestrians it must be removed and this It is a charity to others, which you can provide people with good things or deeds.

Charity money in Islam does not decrease the money, rather it increases because God Almighty opens doors of goodness for you that you did not know.

Teaching self-control

Ramadan in which a Muslim learns to control his desires, in Ramadan a Muslim refrains from eating, drinking and intercourse with his wife from sunrise until sunset, and he learns to control his actions because God commanded us in this month not to do something as bad as insulting or quarrels, for example if a Muslim is insulted from Someone does not exchange him with insults, the Muslim must control himself and say God, I am fasting, in any case, the Muslim does not utter insults, but rather tries to mend his relationship with people, and people only see goodness from him.

Health benefits

Fasting also has benefits for human health and is proven by experimental science.

Zakat Eid al-Fitr

In the last two days of Ramadan, people provide assistance to the needy, this assistance is called "Zakat Eid al-Fitr", in which people provide food and money to those they can't celebrate Eid because have no food or money at the day of Eid, this is the Islam, a social solidarity debt.

Eid al-Fitr

Ramadan ends when people see the crescent of the month of Shawwal, the first day of the month of Shawwal is the holiday called Eid Al Fitr.

On the day of Eid, early morning at the time of a prayer called Eid prayer, people gather somewhere and then begin to repeat the takbeers:

الله أكبر، الله أكبر، الله أكبر، لا إله إلا الله، الله أكبر، الله أكبر ولله الحمد. الله أكبر كبيراً، والحمد لله كثيراً، وسبحان الله بكرةً وأصيلا.

God is great, God is great, God is great, there is no god but God, God is great, God is great and praise be to God. God is great, praise be to God a lot, and glory be to God, by the way.

Eid al-Fitr

They pray two rakats and then listen to the sermon of the imam, then they separate and celebrations begin, visiting relatives and giving money and gifts to the children.

Conditions of Fasting

1_Obligation terms

The Islam:

To be a Muslim, a non-Muslim fast is not valid.

The mind:

Fasting is not valid for a crazy.

The puberty:

Fasting is not obligatory for a boy.

The residence:

The traveler is not obligated, but he must break his fast.

The ability:

It is not necessary to fast for someone who has a disease that prevents him from abstaining from eating and drinking such as diabetes.

For example, in some cases, diabetics cannot tolerate hunger and thirst.

2_fasting to be correct

The intention:

A person intends to fast at night.

Fasting time:

Not valid in the forbidden days as the day of Eid.

Purification of menstruation and postpartum blood is not valid for a woman's fasting in this case.

Making up for days that you do not fast during Ramadan

Making up lost fasting days

He who breaks the fast in Ramadan for a legitimate excuse, such as sickness, travel, or other things, he must to make up what he did not fast, according to the number of days that he did not fast.no fidya or kaffarah in this case.

Fidya

For people cannot make up the missed fast days, they may have a chronic disease(for example),they should pay fidya.

_The amount of the Fidya is according to the country of residence.

Kaffarah

For people that break the fast without a valid reason.

-they must fast continuously for 60 days.
Or
_they must to feed 60 poor people .

Dua for breaking fast

كَانَ رَسُولُ اللَّهِ صلى الله عليه وسلم إِذَا أَفْطَرَ قَالَ
" ذَهَبَ الظَّمَأُ وَابْتَلَّتِ الْعُرُوقُ وَثَبَتَ الْأَجْرُ إِنْ شَاءَ اللَّهُ "

dhahb alzzama , wabtllat alerwq wthabat alajr 'in sha' allh

---

the Prophet (ﷺ) said when he broke his fast:
Thirst has gone, the arteries are moist, and the reward
is sure, if Allah wills.

24

The Etiquette of Eating

عن عمر بن أبي سلمة رضى الله عنهما قال: قال لي رسول الله صلى الله عليه وسلم:
"سم الله وكل بيمينك، وكل مما يليك"

'Umar bin Abu Salamah (May Allah be pleased with him) reported:
Messenger of Allah (ﷺ), said to me, "Mention Allah's Name (i.e., say Bismillah before starting eating), eat with your right hand, and eat from what is near you."

The Etiquette of Eating

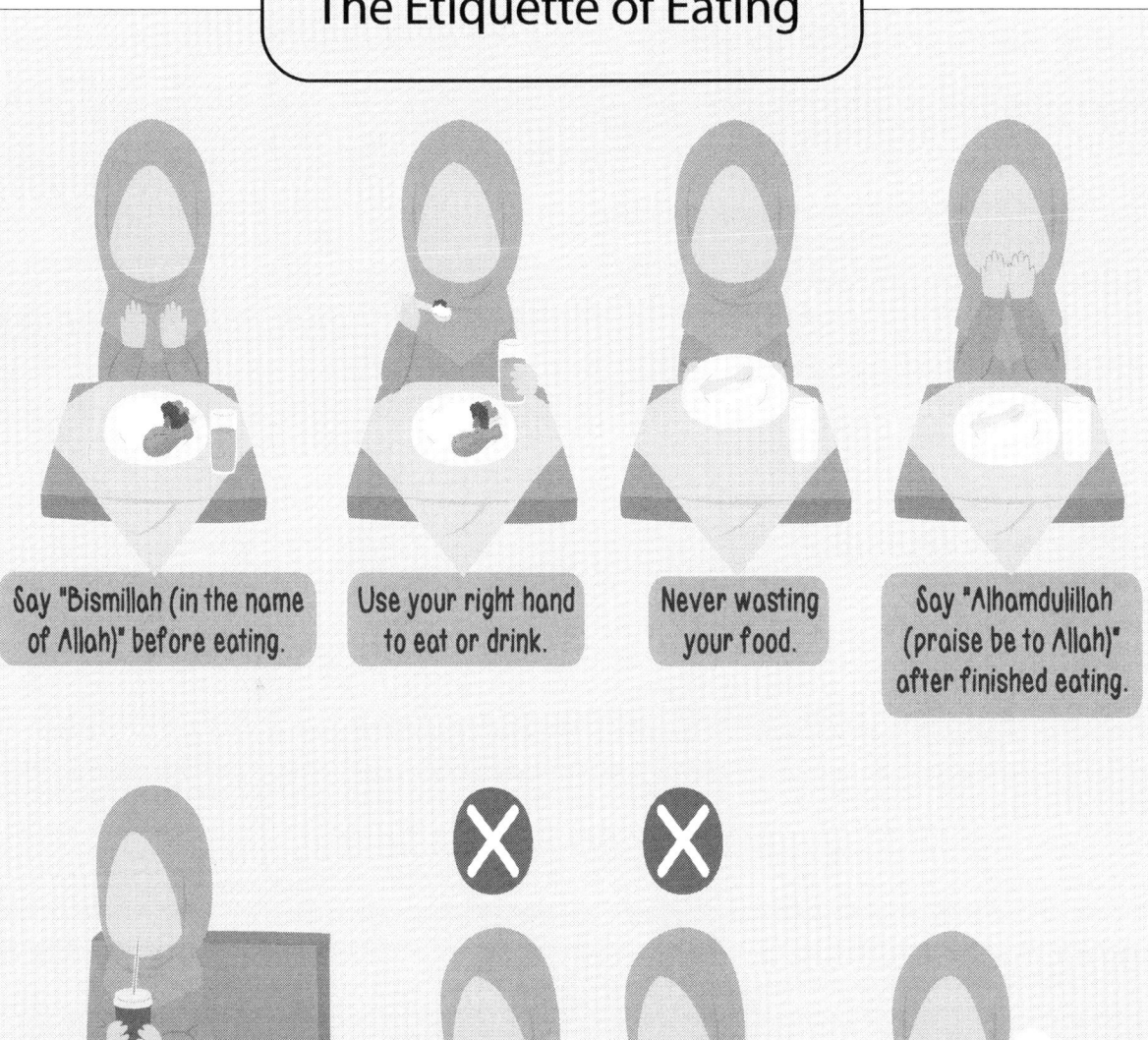

Say "Bismillah (in the name of Allah)" before eating.

Use your right hand to eat or drink.

Never wasting your food.

Say "Alhamdulillah (praise be to Allah)" after finished eating.

Be seated while eating or drinking.

Do not blowing over hot food or drink. Wait for it to cool down.

Make sure every food is "Halal" to consume.

Morning Dua

أَصْبَحْنا وَأَصْبَحْ المُلك لله رَبِّ العـالَمـين ، اللّهُـمَّ إنِّي أسـألُكَ خَـيْرَ هـذا اليَوْم ، فَتْحَهُ ، وَنَصْرَهُ ، وَنـورَهُ وَبَرَكَتَهُ ، وَهُـداهُ ، وَأعـوذُ بِـكَ مِـنْ شَـرِّ ما فيهِ وَشَـرِّ ما بَعْـدَه

'asbahna wa'asbah almulk llh rabi alealamyn , alllhuma 'iiniy as'aluk khayr hdha alyawm , fathah , wanasrah , wanwrah wabarakatah , wahudah , wa'aewdh bik min shari ma fyh washari ma baedah

---

The morning has come to me and the whole universe belongs to Allah, the Lord of the worlds, O Allah, I ask of you the good of the day, it's success and aid and it's nur (celestial light) and barakaat (blessings) and seek hidayah (guidance) and seek refuge from the evil in it (this day) and from the evil of that which is to come later.

Evening Dua

أَمْسَيْنَا وَأَمْسَى الْمُلْكُ لِلَّهِ وَالْحَمْدُ لِلَّهِ لاَ إِلَهَ إِلاَّ اللَّهُ وَحْدَهُ لاَ شَرِيكَ لَهُ

'amsayna wa'amsaa almulk lillah walhamd lillah
la 'iilah 'iila alllah wahdah la sharik lah

We entered upon evening and the whole Kingdom of Allah also entered upon evening and praise is due to Allah. There is no god but Allah, the One Who has no partner with Him.

Method and Dua Of Sleep

رَسُولَ اللَّهِ صلى الله عليه وسلم قَالَ " إِذَا أَوَى أَحَدُكُمْ إِلَى فِرَاشِهِ فَلْيَأْخُذْ دَاخِلَةَ إِزَارِهِ فَلْيَنْفُضْ بِهَا فِرَاشَهُ وَلْيُسَمِّ اللَّهَ فَإِنَّهُ لاَ يَعْلَمُ مَا خَلَفَهُ بَعْدَهُ عَلَى فِرَاشِهِ فَإِذَا أَرَادَ أَنْ يَضْطَجِعَ فَلْيَضْطَجِعْ عَلَى شِقِّهِ الأَيْمَنِ وَلْيَقُلْ سُبْحَانَكَ اللَّهُمَّ رَبِّي بِكَ وَضَعْتُ جَنْبِي وَبِكَ أَرْفَعُهُ إِنْ أَمْسَكْتَ نَفْسِي فَاغْفِرْ لَهَا وَإِنْ أَرْسَلْتَهَا فَاحْفَظْهَا بِمَا تَحْفَظُ بِهِ عِبَادَكَ الصَّالِحِينَ "

subhanak alllahumm rabbi bik wadaet janbi wabik 'arfaeuh 'iin 'amsakt nafsi faghfir laha wa'iin 'arsaltaha fahfazha bima tahfaz bih eibadak alssalihin

---

Allah's Messenger (ﷺ) said

When any one of you goes to bed, he should take hold of the hem of his lower garment and then should clean (his bed) with the help of that and then should recite the name of Allah for he himself does tiot know what he left behind him on his bed, and when he intends to lie on bed, he should lie on his right side and utter these words:" Hallowed be Allah, my Lord. It is with Thine (grace) that I place my side (upon the bed) and it is with Thee that I take it up (after sleep), and in case Thou withholdst my being (if thou causest me to die), then grant pardon to my being, and if Thou keepst (this process of breathing on), then protect it with that with which Thou protected Thine pious servants."

Waking up Dua

الحمدُ لله الذي عافاني في جَسَدي وَرَدّ عَليّ روحي وَأَذِنَ لي بِذِكْرِه.

alhmd llh aladhi eafani fi jasady warad ealy ruwhi wa'adhin li bidhikrih.

All praise is due to Allah, Who healed me in my body, and returned to me my soul, and permitted me to remember Him.

Entering the lavatory Dua

اَللَّهُمَّ إِنِّي أَعُوذُ بِكَ مِنْ الْخُبْثِ وَالْخَبَائِثِ

allahum 'iiniy 'aeudh bik min alkhabth walkhabayith

The Prophet (ﷺ) on entering the lavatory used to say: [Allahumma inni a'udhu bika minal khubthi wal khaba'ithi] "O Allah, I seek refuge with You from devils – males and females (or all offensive and wicked things, evil deeds and evil spirits, etc.)"

Daily Adkar & Dua

عَنِ النَّبِيِّ صلى الله عليه وسلم قَالَ " كَلِمَتَانِ خَفِيفَتَانِ عَلَى اللِّسَانِ، ثَقِيلَتَانِ فِي الْمِيزَانِ، حَبِيبَتَانِ إِلَى الرَّحْمَنِ، سُبْحَانَ اللَّهِ الْعَظِيمِ، سُبْحَانَ اللَّهِ وَبِحَمْدِهِ ".

Subhan Allah Al- `Azim and 'Subhan Allah wa bihamdihi

The Prophet (ﷺ) said, "There are two expressions which are very easy for the tongue to say, but they are very heavy in the balance and are very dear to The Beneficent (Allah), and they are,

"How perfect Allah is and I praise Him; and How perfect Allah is the Most Great."

For any inquiry or note,
please feel free to contact us at:

mohamed.alaoui.publishing@gmail.com

Printed in Great Britain
by Amazon

Lightning Source UK Ltd.
Milton Keynes UK
UKOW05f0736060916

282310UK00009B/212/P